Faculty Freedoms and Institutional Accountability:
Interactions and Conflicts

by Steven G. Olswang and Barbara A. Lee

ASHE-ERIC Higher Education Research Report No. 5, 1984

Prepared by

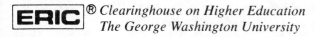 ® *Clearinghouse on Higher Education*
The George Washington University

Published by

Association for the Study of Higher Education

Jonathan D. Fife,
Series Editor

Cite as:
Olswang, Steven G., and Lee, Barbara A. *Faculty Freedoms and Institutional Accountability: Interactions and Conflicts*. ASHE-ERIC Higher Education Research Report No. 5. Washington, D.C.: Association for the Study of Higher Education, 1984.

The ERIC Clearinghouse on Higher Education invites individuals to submit proposals for writing monographs for the Higher Education Research Report series. Proposals must include:
1. A detailed manuscript proposal of not more than five pages.
2. A 75-word summary to be used by several review committees for the initial screening and rating of each proposal.
3. A vita.
4. A writing sample.

Library of Congress Catalog Card Number: 84-73305
ISSN 0737-1292
ISBN 0-913317-14-4

ERIC' **Clearinghouse on Higher Education**
The George Washington University
One Dupont Circle, Suite 630
Washington, D.C. 20036

ASHE **Association for the Study of Higher Education**
One Dupont Circle, Suite 630
Washington, D.C. 20036

This publication was partially prepared with funding from the National Institute of Education, U.S. Department of Education, under contract no. 400-82-0011. The opinions expressed in this report do not necessarily reflect the positions or policies of NIE or the Department.

EXECUTIVE SUMMARY

For nearly three-quarters of a century, academic freedom has protected college faculty in the United States from external control over or inquiry into their teaching methods, the content of their classroom lectures, and the research topics they choose to investigate. Tenure, a legally enforceable set of procedural protections created to secure faculty academic freedom, insulates faculty against most of the traditional sources of external interference, such as a benefactor's discomfort with faculty views, governmental scrutiny of faculty political behavior, or attempts to suppress the teaching of certain doctrines or philosophies.

The increasingly complex environment in which colleges and universities now operate, however, has spawned a set of requirements for accountability with which institutions, and through them faculty, must comply. Faculty are being required to account for the allocation of their time among teaching, service, and research projects to satisfy funding agencies' requirements that the recipients of grants devote the appropriate amount of time to the project. Limitations are being enacted on the amount of time faculty may spend (and, in some cases, the amount of money that can be earned) in outside consulting. Faculty relationships with students are becoming a legal and a moral issue on campus. The rapidity with which these requirements have arrived on campus, and their pervasiveness, suggest a clash with the traditional academic freedom and autonomy enjoyed by college faculty.

How Free Are Faculty?

Academic freedom and tenure provide important protections to faculty members; they are of special importance to the maintenance of the intellectual vitality and creativity of American colleges and universities. Tenure ensures the economic security of the professor and guarantees that due process will be afforded the faculty member should the position be threatened.

While academic freedom and tenure provide important protections, those protections are not unlimited, and faculty with tenure can be removed for cause or in times of financial distress. For example, academic freedom protects faculty from retaliation for the expression of unpopular political or religious beliefs, but it does not immunize faculty against charges of insubordination, neglect of duty, or interference with the efficient operation of the institution. Teaching and classroom discussion are protected by academic freedom, but incompetence is not. Faculty choice of research topics and methodologies is covered by academic freedom, but research fraud or other forms of dishonesty in designing, conducting, and reporting research do not fall under the protections of academic freedom. And while academic freedom permits a faculty member to exercise all the rights that other citizens enjoy, it does not forgive the violation of civil or criminal laws, the abuse of students, gross insubordination, and private misconduct, often labeled "moral turpitude."

How Does Institutional Accountability Affect the Regulation of Faculty Conduct?

Institutions today face a myriad of new pressures and responsibilities. Foremost among them is the need to account for monies received from private donors, state legislatures, and grantors, including private industry, the federal government, and foundations. To meet these heightened responsibilities, institutions are developing new measures of faculty work and implementing new regulations over faculty time and effort.

Several areas in particular have been the focus of institutional rule making. Because faculty outside work performed during the academic year is viewed by the external business community as subsidized competition and by state legislators as a form of double dipping, institutions have enacted limitations on permissible levels of outside consulting. The most common practice is to limit remunerated consulting to no more than one day per calendar week. Consulting in excess of this limitation has been held to be a valid basis for termination of appointment.

The regulation of faculty members' internal workloads is also increasing, and failure by faculty to accept assignments or faculty members' disruption of the internal management of an institution has resulted in dismissals for insubordination. The prohibitions on use of inappropriate criteria for academic decisions, such as those that fall into the category of sexual harassment, further circumscribe the internal conduct of faculty.

Driven by the need for more revenue and a fair financial return for providing a conducive and creative environment, colleges are increasingly exercising their rights of legal ownership over the work product of faculty. Inventions that may be patented and software that may be copyrighted no longer solely belong to the creator or author but are the property rights of the university. The potentially lucrative arrangements between industry and the inventive faculty member also generate an institutional concern over conflict of interest.

Why Review Faculty Performance?

The pressures to regulate faculty time, effort, and behavior also force institutions to examine the substantive performance of faculty. Simply fulfilling the objective time requirements of the job does not ensure quality of performance in assigned duties. The most common criticism of tenure is that it provides a sinecure for the incompetent faculty member.

Periodic review of faculty members' performance in teaching, research, and service is one answer to the increasing demand that faculty competence be examined. It is one way for institutions to document that the expenditure of salary funds is proper and to guarantee to students that the education they receive is of appropriate quality. Evaluating the continued competence of faculty does not infringe on faculty freedoms as competence is a condition of tenure.

How Does Accountability Affect the Institutional Environment?

Colleges and universities, in response primarily to external constituencies, are being compelled to promulgate and enforce limitations in areas of traditional faculty autonomy. Regulations governing outside consulting, conflict of interest, ownership of patents and copyrights, sexual harassment, and periodic reviews of faculty competence all may be perceived to confine the traditional freedoms of faculty. Moreover, violations of these rules become valid cause for the discipline or dismissal of faculty. The overall effect of increasing regulation makes higher education a less desirable environment in which to work.

Intrinsic factors such as autonomy and freedom contribute most to faculty satisfaction. Yet while these new limitations may be legal, necessary, and not technically inconsistent with academic freedom as it has evolved, they do seriously affect job satisfaction. The need to adopt such rules is unavoidable, however, and the answer to lessening their negative impact must therefore lie in the manner in which the rules are formulated and adopted.

Faculty should be actively involved in the creation or modification of institutional policies or structures designed to address requirements for accountability. Joint faculty/administrative groups should discuss and resolve the following issues if these new demands for accountability are to be resolved with minimum resentment from the faculty:

- institutional priorities for academic programming
- the parameters of full-time faculty work and the institution's expectations for faculty productivity
- the institution's method of overseeing faculty research contracts to prevent conflicts of interest
- the regulation of faculty/student interaction and the prevention of instances of sexual harassment
- the institution's procedures for responding to an allegation of fraud in research
- the institution's stance regarding research products that have the potential for returning a profit to the patent or copyright holder
- the design and implementation of a complete system of faculty performance evaluation
- the development of a mechanism that will stimulate continued attention to and discussion of issues of professional ethics, academic accountability, and academic freedom.

Virginia B. Nordby
Director
Affirmative Action Programs
University of Michigan

Eugene Oliver
Director, University Office of School & College Relations
University of Illinois–Champaign

Harold Orlans
Office of Programs and Policy
United States Civil Rights Commission

Marianne Phelps
Assistant Provost for Affirmative Action
The George Washington University

Gary K. Probst
Professor of Reading
Prince Georges Community College

Robert A. Scott
Director of Academic Affairs
State of Indiana Commission for Higher Education

Cliff Sjogren
Director of Admissions
University of Michigan

Al Smith
Assistant Director of the Institute of Higher Education &
    Professor of Instructional Leadership & Support
University of Florida

Donald Williams
Professor of Higher Education
University of Washington

CONTENTS

FOREWORD

During the next decade there will be growing conflict between the goals of a college or university and the freedom of faculty to operate as independent scholars. Properly handled, this situation will be constructive and work for the best interest of the institution. Improperly handled, it will produce lower morale and open hostility that will be disfunctional to an institution's operation.

An institution's goals and administrative procedures are increasingly affected by external as well as internal pressures. Externally, state legislators demand greater accountability for faculty performance. Internally, decreasing resources demand increased faculty productivity; more complicated bureaucratic structures demand more faculty involvement in committee service; and greater percentages of high-ranking tenured faculty suggest a demand for post-tenure review.

On the faculty side, these pressures are interpreted as an erosion of academic prerogatives and a genuine threat to academic freedom and tenure. Post-tenure review is viewed as a major threat to what has been considered as the granting of "life-time" employment. Increased committee assignments are regarded as an imposition on time that could be spent on scholarship. And as faculty salaries fail to keep up with private industry salaries, faculty more frequently seek outside consulting positions to supplement their incomes. At the same time that faculty increase personal income through creative scholarly entrepreneurship, they risk conflict of interest and questions as to who "owns" that scholarship.

In this report by Steven G. Olswang of the University of Washington and Barbara A. Lee of Rutgers, The State University of New Jersey, the varied issues surrounding academic freedom and institutional accountability are clearly articulated. It matters not that both sides—the institution and faculty—have real pressures motivating them to take their respective positions. What is important is that acceptable procedures be developed to minimize this conflict. In order to do this there must be full understanding of situations that motivate institutions and faculty to take the positions they do. This report clarifies these issues and will help both faculty and administrators establish policy that

---

respects not only the principles of academic freedom, but also institutional mission.

Jonathan D. Fife
Series Editor
Professor and Director
ERIC Clearinghouse on Higher Education
The George Washington University

ACKNOWLEDGMENTS

Special acknowledgment is owed several important people for their assistance: to Dr. David Leslie, Dr. Donald Williams, and Ms. Karen Zaugg, for their editorial critiques of early and late drafts; to Ms. Karen Trezise, for her processing and reprocessing of the manuscript; to Dr. Jonathan D. Fife, for his patience and direction; and to our respective spouses, Dr. Lesley Olswang and Dr. James Begin, for their understanding, devotion, and inspiration.

INTRODUCTION

One of the primary motivating factors behind the early
refinements of the concepts of academic freedom and tenure, as defined by the American Association of University
Professors (AAUP), was to provide "a sufficient degree of
economic security to make the [teaching] profession attrac-
tive to men and women of ability" (AAUP 1977a). Among
the concerns that led to these developments were authori-
tarian controls placed on the conduct of faculty, restrictions placed on their areas of study, and the potential consequences meted out by presidents and college benefactors
for exercises of academic independence (Metzger 1979).
These institutional practices placed unwarranted restraint
on faculty freedoms (Commission on Academic Tenure
1973).

Academic freedom and tenure continue to provide vital
protections for faculty in institutions of higher education.
The original concerns—punishment for the exercise of the
freedoms of thought and speech—that generated their evolution have substantially diminished, however. The current
application of the Fourteenth Amendment to the U.S. Constitution, evolution of due process, and recent developments in common law contract theory now substantially
protect faculty academic freedoms whether exercised by
faculty within the institution or in their capacity as citizens. In fact, college faculty enjoy broad protections that
employees working in nonacademic organizations, public
and private, do not enjoy (Lee and Olswang *Forthcoming*).

The 1980s have brought new concerns that continuously
challenge the academic freedom and tenure of faculty. The
financial problems of the 1970s and 1980s will continue for
many colleges—for publicly financed institutions depen-
dent on state tax revenues and for private colleges depen-
dent upon tuition, gifts, and endowments. This reduction in
resources is reflected in the stagnation of faculty salary
levels and in the reductions of available positions for faculty overall (Mingle and Associates 1981; Shulman 1979).
The pressures that young faculty in particular feel to produce accentuates the feeling of frustration (Austin and
Gamson 1983).

These new economic realities have dramatically increased the demand by funding agencies and states to control the use of the funds given to higher education. Institutions are being inundated with requirements to account for

*The 1980s
have brought
new concerns
that . . .
challenge the
academic
freedom and
tenure of
faculty.*

monies they receive. An extreme though pervasive example of these oppressive requirements is the faculty effort reports demanded under the federal government's funding guidelines [OMB *Circular A-21* (44 Fed. Reg. 12368 et seq.)]. States are requiring that the monies laid out for education be justified in terms of their cost effectiveness (Bowen 1974; Peterson, Ervin, and Wilson 1977). In response to these ever-increasing controls and the extended institutional bureaucratization, faculty are exerting their own mechanisms for self-protection, including turning to new mechanisms of governance to bargain for their own rights (Baldridge, Kemerer, and Associates 1981; Lee 1978; Mortimer and Lozier 1974a).

The growing quantity and ferocity of accountability requirements from the states that fund them, the federal government, which authorizes and pays for contract and grant research, and foundations and alumni, which provide discretionary funds, increase the pressure on institutions to ensure that faculty members' performance is adequate. But actions taken by institutions to achieve faculty accountability can potentially infringe on individual autonomy, freedom, and tenure. These demands for accountability do not solely control monetary expenditures, however; they also encompass certain societal goals that higher education and faculty are expected to meet (Astin 1974; Crosson 1983). Thus, these new accountability requirements, as legal responsibilities of the institution, must be examined in juxtaposition with traditional faculty rights and the legal protections afforded those rights by state law, contract, or the Constitution.

Because of the expansion of institutional requirements for accountability, new structures may be created that would substantially change the status of tenure as a protective mechanism. Alternatives to tenure are discussed more and more often in the literature (Baratz 1980; Chait and Ford 1982), but faculty freedoms and tenure need not be sacrificed in the name of accountability. Freedoms, tenure, and accountability are not incompatible. Nonetheless, tenure itself must evolve to be responsive to the future demands placed upon colleges and universities if it is to preserve its original purpose—that of protecting academic freedom and the faculty's right to exercise that freedom.

*Tenure's real concern is with arbitrary or retaliatory
dismissals based on an administrator's or a trustee's
distaste for the content of a professor's teaching or research, or even for positions taken completely outside
the campus setting. . . . It is designed to foster our society's interest in the unfettered progress of research and
learning by protecting the profession's freedom of inquiry and instruction . . . [Browzin v. Catholic University,* 527 F.2d 843 (D.C. Cir. 1975), p. 846].

This report first explores the evolution of academic freedom and tenure, then some of the emerging issues that
require heightened accountability by institutions and individuals. It then relates this institutional responsibility to be
accountable to its various constituencies to the traditional
concepts of academic freedom and tenure to determine
whether or not the emerging requirements are compatible
and where they conflict. Finally, the report projects the
outcomes of such potential conflicts and recommends systems and procedures that should be enacted to avoid undue
and unnecessary problems between faculty and administration while preserving the important concepts of academic
freedom and tenure.

ACADEMIC FREEDOM AND TENURE

Academic freedom and tenure are two of the most widely discussed and vigorously debated concepts in higher education. Although they have been central to the value system of American academic institutions for nearly three-quarters of a century, disputes over the extent of the protections they provide and their philosophical underpinnings flourish today (Chait and Ford 1982; Winerip 1984).

Because of the continuing debate over the scope of academic freedom and a parallel, but conceptually different, debate over the importance of and scope of protections afforded under tenure, it is important to review the origins of academic freedom and to explicate its relationship to tenure. For it is in the origins and development of academic freedom that the protections, as well as the limitations, afforded to academic freedom through tenure become evident.

Development of Academic Freedom

Early precursors to the American strain of academic freedom began in the universities of medieval Europe. The "academic freedom" afforded college faculty in those medieval universities was much more limited than modern academic freedom, however. Although the faculty of medieval universities enjoyed substantial autonomy from external interference (and in fact wielded much political power because they were protected by the popes and emperors), the intellectual freedom of the faculty was sharply limited (Wieruszowski 1966). The religious orthodoxy of the time, combined with the inseparability of state religion and government, limited the ability of academics to express beliefs or findings contrary to the prevailing dogma (Hofstadter and Metzger 1955). Thus, the contribution of medieval British, French, and Italian universities to the modern concept of academic freedom was the primacy of the faculty in determining the mission, curriculum, and academic standards of the institution and their autonomy in selecting the institution's leadership.

German universities added another important dimension to the modern concept of academic freedom. Although most university faculty in nineteenth century Germany were civil servants, they enjoyed two forms of academic freedom: *Lernfreiheit,* which guaranteed German faculty an "absence of administrative coercions in the learning situation" (although the concept emphasized primarily students' free choice in selecting courses and attending classes), and *Lehrfreiheit,* which gave to the German faculty member freedom of teaching and freedom of inquiry (Hofstadter and Metzger 1955, p. 386). Both concepts were interpreted, however, as pertaining only to the internal operations of the university; academics were afforded much less freedom outside the university setting.

Historians tracing the development of modern academic freedom emphasize the importance to that concept of concurrent developments in scientific methodology and political liberalism. Hofstadter and Metzger (1955) believe that modern academic freedom is an amalgam of modern science, with its emphasis on the "continuing search for new truths," the development of the free market theory of commerce and its analogy to "free competition among ideas," and the liberalization of political beliefs, which afforded more protection for free speech, freedom of the press, a greater appreciation of pluralism, and more tolerance for different religious beliefs (p. 61). These developments in modern thought, then, provided a social context conducive to a broader concept of academic freedom, with the result that "the assimilation of the values of science made academic freedom an ethic, an affirmative moral position, and not merely a negative condition, the absence of overt restraint" (p. 363).

The American tradition of lay boards of trustees had substantial impact upon institutional governance and academic freedom. Trustees thought of themselves as "the preservers of collegiate virtue" and "look[ed] upon the professors as a band of invaders" (Rudolph 1962, p. 161). At the turn of the twentieth century, the attitudes of trustees, who came primarily from industry and commerce, clashed mightily with the views of scholars, especially social scientists who espoused new and sometimes anti-capitalist views of economics and politics. "A distinguished roster of academicians learned that freedom, as they understood it, had not yet become a part of the understanding of benefactors and governing boards . . ." (Rudolph 1962, p. 414); faculty were terminated for their unpopular ideas in the two decades before the formation of the AAUP (Commission on Academic Tenure 1973; Metzger 1977).

The courts, while looked on today as one of the principal protectors of institutional autonomy and individual academic freedoms (Slaughter 1980, p. 59), were no more sympathetic to the academic freedom of college faculty in the early 1900s than were the trustees (*Harvard Law Review* 1968). At that time, courts tended to view colleges and universities as just another kind of corporation. For example, the *Dartmouth College* case, often cited as an early example of judicial protection for institutional autonomy, more factually resembles an early corporate law case, affirming the autonomy of the corporation from state control, rather than focusing primarily on academic rights [*Trustees of Dartmouth College* v. *Woodward*, 4 Wheat. (U.S.) 518 (1819)]. Similarly, in early academic employment cases, as long as the trustees could establish that in their view the termination of a faculty member's employment was in the college's interest, the courts would usually defer to that judgment and would require only that a "fair hearing" based on common law (rather than constitutional) property rights be afforded the faculty member (Hofstadter and Metzger 1955, p. 463).

In view of the double threat to faculty academic freedom from trustees' intolerance and judicial deference to trustees' authority, a group of college professors from several learned societies met to formulate a general statement on academic freedom. Out of those meetings was born the American Association of University Professors, which in turn produced a statement in 1915 describing the protections to be afforded by academic freedom and the concomitant responsibilities of college faculty (Hofstadter and Metzger 1955). That statement focused upon three elements of academic freedom: (1) freedom of inquiry and research; (2) freedom of teaching within the university; and (3) freedom of extramural utterance and action. Perhaps reacting to the earlier domination by the trustees, the statement asserted that faculty responsibility is "primarily to the public" and to the profession, rather than to institutional boards. The statement is, in fact, a declaration of intellectual independence and autonomy:

University teachers should be understood to be, with respect to the conclusions reached and expressed by them, no more subject to the control of the trustees, than are judges subject to the control of the President, with respect to their decisions; while of course, for the same reason, trustees are no more to be held responsible for, or to be presumed to agree with, the opinions or utterances of professors, than the President can be assumed to approve of all the legal reasonings by the courts (AAUP 1916, p. 26).

The founders of the AAUP simultaneously proclaimed the responsibilities of faculty that accompany this academic freedom: fairness and honesty in conducting and reporting research, the maintenance of professional standards, the importance of avoiding indoctrination or its appearance, and temperance in extramural utterances. The drafters of the statement made a special effort to disassociate academic freedom from the protection of incompetence:

If this profession should prove itself unwilling to purge its ranks of the incompetent and the unworthy, or to prevent the freedom which it claims in the name of science from being used as a shelter for inefficiency, for superficiality, or for uncritical and intemperate partisanship, it is certain that the task will be performed by others (AAUP 1916, p. 34).

This early statement defined tenure primarily as a mechanism to protect academic freedom in its provision of procedural guarantees to individuals whose employment was threatened because of their espousal of unpopular ideas. One historian has argued that the professors who drafted the early AAUP statements, conscious of their dependency upon their universities, "consistently sacrificed individual and substantive principles in order to gain compliance for procedural safeguards from university officials for the profession as a whole" (Slaughter 1980, pp. 47–48). Although the Statement of Principles acknowledged the importance of economic security to the protection of academic freedom, its use of tenure was viewed as a means to protecting academic freedom rather than as an end in itself.

Scope of Academic Freedom
The scope of academic freedom was originally defined in policy statements formulated by the AAUP, though more

recently the courts have played an important role in defining its meaning and protections. Probably the most widely used articulation of the scope of academic freedom is the AAUP's 1940 statement on academic freedom and tenure. That statement addresses freedom in research and publication, freedom in the classroom, and freedom in extramural activities. Yet like its predecessor statements, it includes important limitations to these freedoms. The professor is expected to maintain "adequate performance" of academic duties, to refrain from including in his or her teaching "controversial matter which has no relation to his subject," and to "exercise appropriate restraint [and] . . . show respect for the opinions of others" in extramural utterances (AAUP 1977a, p. 3).

The 1940 statement's definition of academic freedom is particularly important because courts have used it to establish the employment rights of college faculty who have been disciplined or whose employment has been terminated (Lee and Olswang *Forthcoming*). At institutions that have incorporated the 1940 statement or other AAUP statements into faculty handbooks or other policy documents, courts have ruled that such policies are part of the college's employment contract with the faculty member. Even when institutions have not explicitly incorporated AAUP statements into their policy documents, courts will often hold colleges and universities responsible for complying with the practices required by these statements, interpreting them as a kind of "industry practice" based on widely held norms and beliefs [Miller 1981; *Greene* v. *Howard University*, 412 F.2d 1128 (D.C. Cir. 1969)].

The courts have been careful, however, to define with some precision the kinds of faculty behavior that are protected and the conduct that is not under the concept of academic freedom (Lovain 1983–84). Judicial protection has been given to faculty conduct in four areas: individual political and religious beliefs, teaching and classroom activities, research and inquiry, and the conduct of one's private affairs, both as a citizen and as a member of a learned profession.

Political and religious beliefs

The courts have been most active in the area of protecting the individual political and religious beliefs of faculty against pressure for conformity or orthodoxy by administrators, trustees, legislators, or others. In an early case, *Sweezy* v. *New Hampshire,* the U.S. Supreme Court recognized academic freedom as a constitutionally protected right, ruling that "[t]eachers and students must always remain free to inquire, to study, and to evalute, to gain new maturity and understanding" [354 U.S. 234 (1957), p. 250]. In *Sweezy,* a professor had refused to testify before the New Hampshire legislature about the content of a lecture delivered to a class at the University of New Hampshire; the state inquiry into his political beliefs and affiliations was found to violate the Fourteenth Amendment of the Constitution (". . . nor shall any state deprive any person of life, liberty, or property, without due process of law"). While the Court's opinions expound at some length about the importance of academic freedom to the strength of higher education institutions, the court based its ruling on two concepts: the political freedom guaranteed every individual under the U.S. Constitution that must be equally afforded to faculty, and the special need of college and university faculty for protection from external governmental coercion.

> *To impose any strait jacket upon the intellectual leaders in our colleges and universities would imperil the future of our nation. No field of education is so thoroughly comprehended by man that new discoveries cannot yet be made. . . . Scholarship cannot flourish in an atmosphere of suspicion and distrust (Sweezy 1957, p. 250).*

Other cases involving academic freedom arose in the context of loyalty oaths that professors were required to sign as a condition of employment at public colleges and universities. The courts struck all but the most general of these loyalty oaths, saying that they violated the Constitution's First Amendment, which "does not tolerate laws that cast a pall of orthodoxy over the classroom" [*Keyishian* v. *Board of Regents*, 385 U.S. 589 (1967), p. 603]. Thus, the courts strongly endorsed the importance of a faculty member's right to hold political views different from those who oversee or operate the institution (Van Alstyne 1970).

Not all faculty were afforded the same degree of judicial protection as were Messrs Sweezy and Keyishian, however. Between 1949 and 1955, at the height of the McCarthy era, the AAUP has calculated that at least 77 professors were dismissed for their political activism (Slaughter 1980, p. 58). In a number of those cases, institutions alleged that "subversive" political activity impaired the faculty member's ability to perform his or her teaching responsibilities, an allegation that, if sustained by the courts, cannot be overborne by academic freedom protections.

Judicial protection for individual political views has not been extended to disruptive activities by college faculty, however. In *Adamian* v. *Jacobsen* [523 F.2d 929 (9th Cir. 1975)], a federal court upheld the University of Nevada's decision to terminate the tenured employment of a faculty member who led a protest march that disrupted an institutional ceremony. A faculty committee hearing his case had found that the professor violated an institutional rule requiring faculty at the university to "show respect for the opinions of others," a phrase taken directly from the AAUP's 1940 statement (p. 932). The professor whose employment had been terminated alleged that such a regulation was an impermissible restraint on free speech and a violation of his academic freedom. According to the AAUP's own interpretation of these words, the regulation applied only to "serious intemperateness of expression, incitement of misconduct, or conceivably some other impropriety of circumstances" rather than in the unpopularity of the idea expressed (p. 934). The court ruled that, if the university could establish that its interpretation of the disputed rule complied with the narrow AAUP interpretation, then such a rule was a legitimate regulation of the time, place, and manner of speech, rather than a restriction on the faculty member's academic freedom. Upon a subsequent judicial determination that Professor Adamian was fired for inciting misconduct rather than for the unpopular ideas he expressed, the dismissal was found to be permissible.

Although faculty criticism of the administration is clearly protected by academic freedom [*Smith* v. *Losee*, 485 F.2d 334 (10th Cir. 1973)], faculty conduct that becomes bellig-

Judicial protection for individual political views has not been extended to disruptive activities by college faculty.

erent and uncooperative may no longer be protected by the
First Amendment freedoms of speech [*Jawa* v. *Fayetteville
State University*, 426 F. Supp. 218 (E.D.N.C. 1976)].
Courts examine the faculty conduct carefully in cases
where insubordination is alleged because of the potential
for violations of First Amendment and academic freedom
rights. If, however, the college can establish that sufficient
misconduct exists that is *not* protected by the First
Amendment or academic freedom, courts will uphold the
dismissal [*Mt. Healthy* v. *Doyle*, 419 U.S. 274 (1977)]. One
court observed that "academic freedom is not a license for
activity at variance with job-related procedures and requirements, nor does it encompass activities which are
internally destructive to the proper function of the university or disruptive to the education process" [*Stastny* v.
Board of Trustees of Central Washington University, 647
P.2d 496 (Wash. App. 1982), p. 504]. The mere fact that
"noncooperation and aggressive behavior are verbalized"
does not immunize the faculty member from the loss of his
job, nor does it bring the conduct within the protections of
academic freedom [*Chitwood* v. *Feaster*, 468 F.2d 359 (4th
Cir. 1972), p. 360].

Although political and other individual beliefs continue
to receive considerable protection under both academic
freedom and the First Amendment, these protections are
not absolute. While both the First Amendment and academic freedom were designed to protect the rights of individuals with unpopular or minority viewpoints, group pressure on college campuses has occasionally resulted in
prohibiting a scientist from speaking or cutting short the
lecture of an unpopular government official (Finn 1984;
Jensen 1983). In fact, one scholar has concluded that "academic freedom is in some jeopardy on our campuses, not
so much because of malign constraints imposed from without as because of decay within" (Finn 1984, p. 49). Despite
this dismal view of the protective powers of academic freedom, however, individual conduct that does not impair a
professor's ability to perform his or her job receives considerable protection.

Teaching and classroom discussion
A second area where the protections afforded by academic
freedom are generally recognized is in the faculty mem-

ber's teaching and other classroom activities. *Sweezy* established a professor's freedom to discuss a controversial subject in class without regulation by the university. Furthermore, faculty members are protected by academic freedom against retaliatory dismissal if part of their legitimate classroom or other teaching activity includes criticism of the college administration. For example, a professor of journalism who was fired after she wrote an editorial for the student newspaper discussing potential conflicts of interest involving trustees was reinstated after the court found the dismissal to have violated both her First Amendment right of free speech and academic freedom [*Endress* v. *Brookdale Community College*, 364 A.2d 1080 (N.J. Super. A.D. 1976)]. There are boundaries to the amount of protection for classroom activities that courts will afford, however. In *Hetrick* v. *Martin*, a state university refused to renew the contract of a nontenured faculty member because the administration disapproved of her "pedagogical attitude" [480 F.2d 705 (6th Cir. 1973)]. Both students and their parents had complained about certain remarks the professor had made in her English class, including discussions of the war in Vietnam. The court did not view the university's action as a violation of academic freedom but as a legitimate decision concerning the teaching methods and philosophies considered appropriate for that institution.

Although it is widely believed that academic freedom and tenure protect incompetent faculty members from dismissal, colleges alleging incompetence as the reason for dismissing tenured faculty members that can document that incompetence prevail in court in the overwhelming proportion of cases (Lovain 1983–84, p. 422). Courts have upheld the right of colleges and universities to dismiss tenured faculty whose teaching was poor [*Chung* v. *Park*, 514 F.2d 382 (3d Cir. 1975)] or whose relationships with students and colleagues were unsatisfactory *(Jawa* v. *Fayetteville State University)*. Although several courts have found administrators' allegations of incompetence to be pretexts for dismissing faculty for unpopular beliefs, "where charges of incompetence, especially in teaching, are supported by substantial and relevant evidence, the courts will defer to the expertise of academic administrators" and uphold the dismissal (Lovain 1983–84, p. 423).

The protections of academic freedom are not extended

to what has been called "unrelated utterances" (Zimic 1978), although it would be unusual to find a situation in which the sole ground for dismissal of a faculty member was the incorporation of unrelated material into classroom discussions. The AAUP's 1940 statement cautions against the introduction into classroom discussions of material that has "no relation to [the] subject." If, however, a college alleges that the introduction of unrelated material, in combination with other manifestations of poor teaching, constitutes incompetence or neglect of the duties assigned, academic freedom would not protect that faculty member from dismissal.

Research and scholarship

A third area of protection, that pertaining to research and inquiry, has been especially pertinent in recent years. Although researchers still enjoy broad discretion in selecting their topics of research and the methodologies to be used, flexibility to select specializations and freedom to choose methodologies have been curtailed in recent years. Several branches of government have imposed limitations on the freedom to conduct research. For example, federal funding agencies have issued regulations regarding how human and animal subjects must be treated and have required that institutional review boards be established to evaluate and monitor the methodologies used to experiment with such subjects. Although one might view such regulation as a limitation of individual academic freedom, however, the mechanism used to implement this "limitation" is peer review rather than "interference" by external, nonacademic agents, such as government regulators. Nonetheless, the freedom to inquire has been subjected to limitations.

Despite the heightened regulation of scientific inquiry, strong protection exists for those researchers who comply with the policies of their institutions and their funding agents. Academic researchers won an important victory against premature disclosure of their research results in *Dow Chemical Co.* v. *Allen* [672 F.2d 1262 (7th Cir. 1982)]. Dow Chemical Company, in an attempt to challenge a ruling by the Environmental Protection Agency curtailing the marketing of some of its herbicides, subpoenaed the records of two researchers at the University of Wisconsin who were studying animal toxicity. The research was not complete, and the researchers objected to being required to turn over all their records and to testify about findings and conclusions that were still tentative. The Court of Appeals for the Seventh Circuit ruled that research in academic laboratories is protected by the First Amendment and that a subpoena of the breadth of that in *Dow* tended to "chill the exercise of academic freedom" (p. 1276). Although the court used a balancing test to weigh Dow's need for the data against the interest of the researchers in preserving the integrity of their unfinished research, the court noted the negative consequences of the disclosure demanded by Dow Chemical.

> *Public access would make the studies an unacceptable basis for scientific papers or other research; peer review and publication are crucial to the researchers' credibility and careers and would be precluded by whole or partial public disclosure of the information; and loss of the opportunity to publish would severely decrease the researchers' professional opportunities in the future* (Hoornstra and Liethen 1983–84, p. 127).

It is important to note, however, that this protection was afforded the researchers because Dow could not prove that its need for the data overcame the researchers' academic freedom.

The broad protections of academic freedom for the conduct of research and inquiry apply to the selection of the research topic and the method of study. Early in the development of academic freedom in America, proponents of academic freedom warned that it must not be expanded to shield incompetence or dishonesty in research. Early definitions of academic freedom expressly excluded protection for unethical professional conduct (Murphy 1963, p. 451). Other commentators on the nature and scope of academic freedom have included research fraud within the category of "professional incompetence," a well-recognized cause for dismissal of tenured faculty (Gideonse 1950, p. 96; Machlup 1967b, p. 186). Furthermore, the Commission on Academic Tenure included "dishonesty in teaching or research"as one of the three types of "adequate cause" for the dismissal of tenured faculty (1973, p. 75).

AAUP's "Statement on Professional Ethics" addresses the obligation of college faculty to maintain high standards of integrity in research:

The professor, guided by a deep conviction of the worth and dignity of the advancement of knowledge, recognizes the special responsibilities placed upon him. His primary responsibility to his subject is to seek and to state the truth as he sees it. . . . He accepts the obligation to exercise critical self-discipline and judgment in using, extending, and transmitting knowledge. He practices intellectual honesty (AAUP 1977e, p. 65).

Private misconduct

The Commission on Academic Tenure lists as one of the three "adequate causes" for faculty dismissal "personal conduct which substantially impairs the individual's fulfillment of his institutional responsibilities" (1973, p. 75). Often called "moral turpitude," private misconduct must be linked in some way to a faculty member's performance as a teacher and scholar before it will serve as an appropriate basis for termination (and thus be unprotected by academic freedom).

The term "moral turpitude" is often used to refer to any kind of faculty dishonesty or misconduct deemed to be outside the scope of academic freedom. Moral turpitude generally involves private conduct that is forbidden by law, such as indecent exposure, sexual misconduct, or other criminal charges involving immoral or dishonest conduct. Faculty have been dismissed for committing "immoral acts" with students [*Board of Trustees of Mount San Antonio Junior College* v. *Hartman*, 55 Cal. Rptr. 144 (Ct. App. 1966); *Board of Trustees* v. *Stubblefield*, 94 Cal. Rptr. 318 (Ct. App. 1971)], even if the misconduct occurred off campus with adult students. Inappropriate supervision of minor college students has been found to be immoral conduct sufficient to support dismissal [*White* v. *Board of Trustees of Western Wyoming Community College*, 648 P.2d 528 (Wyo. 1982)]. Unwarranted sexual advances toward students and colleagues have also justified dismissal on the grounds of moral turpitude [*Lehmann* v. *Board of Trustees of Whitman College*, 89 Wash. 2d 874, 576 P.2d 397 (1978)].

Legislative and judicial definitions of moral turpitude differ by state and by the issue involved; what is critical is the link between the misbehavior and the faculty member's ability to perform his or her job. This view of moral turpitude suggests that a wide range of student/faculty interactions (such as sexual harassment) could potentially be included under the rubric of moral turpitude. As it stands now, the concept is only vaguely defined, and more litigation will very likely be necessary to clarify the range of misconduct that can appropriately be termed "moral turpitude."

In summary, academic freedom is the right to conduct one's research and teach one's subjects free of institutional and governmental interference and supervision. This freedom has evolved from earlier times when the espousal of unpopular ideas or theories different from the traditional dogma resulted in the termination of faculty for such acts. Academic freedom grants faculty the ability to speak freely inside and outside the classroom, to express political and religious ideas different from those of his or her employer, and to search out new and different discoveries, no matter how unique or controversial.

All conduct by faculty is not condoned within the concept of academic freedom, however. While courts have afforded faculty broad protections in the performance of their jobs, protection based on academic freedom has been limited in significant ways. Institutions remain free to enforce institutional rules and to expect nondisruptive conduct from their faculty. Faculty retain the obligation to act in a normally ethical manner, both in their individual personal conduct and in the conduct of their research and teaching. Academic freedom, while broad in its scope, is not unlimited in what faculty conduct it will insulate.

Relationship between Academic Freedom and Tenure
Academic freedom, as defined by the commentators and by the courts, is the philosophy or the set of norms and values that protects a faculty member's freedom of intellectual expression and inquiry. Academic freedom is meaningless, however, without a set of legal protections. To that end, tenure has been created to provide a set of procedural protections designed to guard faculty against the negative

consequences of unpopular beliefs on the individual's employment.

Tenure may be awarded under a state statute, pursuant to institutional regulation, or under a contract between the faculty member and the institution. Regardless of whether a statute or a contract confers tenure, however, the concept of tenure generally means that, absent sufficient cause for dismissal, the college must assume that the tenured faculty member will be employed until retirement (Shulman 1973).

While tenure provides job security for faculty until retirement, it was initially designed only to protect those individuals whose conduct is protected by academic freedom. The system of due process protections afforded by tenure provides the faculty member, and the institution, with a method of determining whether the disciplining or dismissal of a tenured faculty member is for conduct outside the scope of academic freedom (making the discipline permissible), or is an unwarranted violation of academic freedom. In other words, tenure affords a process for determining whether certain conduct can permissibly be punished.

Tenured status generally protects a faculty member against dismissal except for reasons of financial exigency, program elimination, or "just cause" (Commission on Academic Tenure 1973) with the specific causes justifying dismissal spelled out in either the statute or the contract (Lovain 1983–84; Weeks 1979). If the contract or statute is silent on the definition of cause, courts have incorporated into the employment relationship the causal bases and protective procedures suggested by the AAUP *(Greene* v. *Howard University* 1969). While certain specific causes have evolved from the AAUP documents and the courts, the AAUP itself defers the definition of cause to the institutions:

> *One persistent source of difficulty is the definition of adequate cause for dismissal of a faculty member. Despite the 1940 Statement of Principles on Academic Freedom and Tenure, and subsequent attempts to build upon it, considerable ambiguity and misunderstanding persists throughout higher education, especially in the respective conceptions of governing boards, administra-*

tive officers, and faculties concerning this matter. The present statement assumes that individual institutions will have formulated their own definitions of adequate cause for dismissal, bearing in mind the 1940 Statement and standards which have been developed in the experience of academic institutions (AAUP 1977d, p. 5).

In general, causes accepted as justifying the dismissal of tenured faculty include incompetence, moral turpitude, neglect of duty, and insubordination (Lovain 1983–84; Olswang and Fantel 1980–81).

When tenure is challenged, academic due process is required to ensure that the reasons are valid and supportable and that they are not a pretext to punish for the legitimate exercise of academic freedom. Academic due process has several components:

1. During the time of informal conciliation, the faculty member should not be suspended unless there is danger of imminent harm to that individual or others.
2. The administration must provide the faculty member with the following: a statement of applicable rules, the charges against the faculty member, a summary of the evidence against him or her, a preliminary list of witnesses, the procedure to be followed during the hearing, and an invitation to bring an advisor.
3. All communications to the faculty member must be in writing.
4. A professor should be permitted to have legal counsel.
5. The hearing committee should be entirely or predominantly made up of faculty members.
6. The burden of proof is on the college (Joughin 1967a, pp. 276–87).

In addition, the faculty member should have the opportunity to confront the witnesses against him or her, to have the hearing recorded and a record of the hearing kept, and a written decision based only upon the evidence presented during the hearing *(Chung* v. *Park* 1975, p. 386).

Although the courts generally require that colleges and universities follow these elements of due process in conducting dismissal hearings [*Ferguson* v. *Thomas*, 430 F.2d

852 (5th Cir. 1970)], courts have been unsympathetic to faculty complaints that the hearings afforded did not resemble court proceedings and thus violated their constitutionally afforded rights of due process. One court stated that "a proceeding may provide a fair and adequate opportunity for the grievant to present his side of the issues without either the legal technicalities of the hearsay rule or the presence of counsel" [*Toney* v. *Reagan,* 467 F.2d 953 (9th Cir. 1972), p. 958]. In general, if the court believes that the college has given the faculty member facing dismissal a fair chance to challenge the reason for dismissal and has carefully examined the evidence presented by all parties, the court will not attempt to assess the accuracy of the decision to dismiss the faculty member. In other words, the courts focus upon the procedural fairness of the tenure hearing rather than upon the substantive basis upon which charges are made against faculty members (Edwards and Nordin 1979, p. 14).

Because the judicial system looks primarily at the procedural protections given the faculty member rather than the sufficiency of the factual basis for the decision, many faculty who believe their employing institutions have violated their academic freedom seek the assistance of the American Association of University Professors. Committee A of the AAUP, made up entirely of college professors, investigates the issues involved in the suspected violation and reports its findings in the association's journal. Between 1970 and 1980, the AAUP received 2,135 complaints from faculty alleging violations of academic freedom (Slaughter 1981, p. 79). Of those complaints, the AAUP staff handled nearly half without a formal investigation, about one-quarter were resolved successfully, and only 2 percent were investigated by Committee A. While a complaint to the AAUP, if investigated by Committee A, receives more scrutiny of the facts surrounding the complaint than a judicial procedure would afford, the remedies available to individuals whose charges are supported by Committee A are more limited than judicial remedies. If Committee A finds that an academic freedom has been violated and the institution so accused is unwilling to settle the dispute, the association will place that institution on its list of "censured" institutions, an act that warns prospective as well as cur-

rent faculty that "the institution so listed does not sub-
scribe to AAUP academic freedom and tenure policies"
(Slaughter 1981, p. 83). Despite the dual protections of
judicially enforced due process and peer group investiga-
tions through the AAUP, Slaughter concludes that they are
inadequate in the face of external political and economic
pressures to reduce the number of academic programs and
thus the size of the faculty. As institutions facing fiscal
pressures make decisions about which programs to close
and which faculty to lay off, "removal of those [faculty]
with ideas defined as extraneous, unorthodox, or controversial might well pass unnoticed and unmourned"
(Slaughter 1981, p. 95).

While researchers like Slaughter address the weaknesses
of such protections, others believe that these protections
are overly generous and that they prevent institutions from
terminating faculty whose performance is unsatisfactory.
That the scope of tenure is coextensive with the scope of
academic freedom and should not protect incompetence,
immorality, or other misconduct has been firmly established by both the courts and the commentators. In
practice, however, such limitations to tenure's protection
have not always been readily perceived, and much has
been written about the evils of tenure in making it difficult
or nearly impossible for institutions to weed out "dead
wood," incompetence, or unprofessional behavior (Chait
and Ford 1982; Nisbet 1978, p. 27; O'Toole 1979; Silber
1973, p. 49). Indeed, this criticism of tenure is a major one:

*Some of the criticisms of tenure are valid, as knowledge-
able and candid proponents of tenure have always ad-
mitted. No system involving the judgment of persons can
ever be foolproof; tenure decisions have on occasion
been wrong and will continue to be. People change as
they grow older; the powers and energies of some will
decline, and some will decide to coast and take it easy.
Institutions wishing to upgrade themselves have in fact
found their efforts impeded by the presence of certain
tenured faculty members, who were perhaps competent
enough by the earlier standards but mediocre by the new*
(Commission on Academic Tenure 1973, pp. 19–20).

Such a widely held perception of tenure serves higher education poorly, for analysis of the judicial treatment of tenure and academic freedom does not support this view (Lee and Olswang *Forthcoming*). This is not to say, however, that critics of tenure are inaccurate; faculty and administrators either do not correctly understand its scope and limitations, or they are unwilling to take the steps to enforce professional ethics and responsible behavior on the part of their colleagues.

> *Tenure is not an invulnerable shield for incompetencies of all kinds. However, we also know that our tenured faculties do contain some colleagues who are no longer meeting their responsibilities, and we also know that while,* de jure, *tenure is not an invulnerable shield,* de facto *the opposite is more nearly the case on most campuses* (Shapiro 1982, p. 4a).

With evolving issues requiring institutions to be more responsive to external and internal calls for accountability, it may well be that institutions' laissez-faire attitude will end.

Summary
While academic freedom and tenure provide important protections to faculty members and are of special importance to the maintenance of the intellectual vitality and creativity of American colleges and universities, these protections are not without boundaries. The courts, the AAUP, and the commentators all stress the inseparability of academic freedom from professional responsibility and ethics. They assert the importance of professional self-regulation and the duty of college faculty to conform to the image of fairness, integrity, and competence implied by the concepts of academic freedom. Tenure was created to protect the essence of academic integrity and the exercise of personal and intellectual freedoms encompassed within these concepts. In light of the implications of academic freedom and tenure, then, the numerous accountability requirements both sought by and being forced upon academe must be assessed as to their conformity and adherence to these principles.

EMERGING INSTITUTIONAL RESPONSIBILITIES AND ACCOUNTABILITIES

Colleges and universities today are faced with a myriad of new requirements and pressures. Among them are reduced funding, general state and federal regulations, effort-reporting requirements, cooperative relationships with the private sector, and internal equity. Such regulation affects institutional autonomy (Berdahl 1971; Finn 1978; Hobbs 1978; McGuiness 1981; Millett 1981; Shulman 1978), and, while each individual regulation is not negative in and of itself, it combines with others to pressure the institution into establishing numerous mechanisms for accountability, which inevitably affect individual faculty members. Pressures from external sources have a negative impact on the working environment of faculty members (Austin and Gamson 1983; Meléndez and de Guzmán 1983).

Emerging institutional responsibilities to external and internal constituencies must be examined and understood. The potential for altering the traditional faculty/university relationship, and thus the rights faculty have exercised under the concepts of academic freedom and tenure, is substantial. Future shifts in institutions' responsibilities will further shape and refine faculty employment rights and responsibilities and thus have implications for academic freedom.

The potential for [external pressures to alter] the traditional faculty/university relationship . . . is substantial.

Financial Reductions

In recent years, higher education has encountered, and in future years will continue to be confronted with, declines in enrollment and in state and private support (Carnegie Council 1980; Glenny and Bowen 1981). While the actual dollar allocation to higher education has increased over the last decades, so has access to higher education. The result has been a severe reduction in the per-student rate of support and a reduction in the percentage of annual growth (Bowen 1978). And while some predict that these financial problems are passing, they still must be addressed (Kerr 1984).

At the same time that revenues were declining and costs rising, shifts in students' demand from liberal arts or other disciplines to business, engineering, and the professions have forced institutions to reassess the distribution of personnel. The response of many institutions was to reduce programs, remove faculty in low-demand areas, or even close when revenues were insufficient. The literature swelled with plans and procedures for faculty and program reductions (Dolan-Greene 1981; Dougherty 1981; Hendrickson and Lee 1983; Olswang 1982–83) or options in these situations (Boulding 1975; Bowen 1982; Neuman 1982).

While being faced with declining revenues and increasing costs, institutions are simultaneously being asked to improve education, provide access to greater numbers of minorities and other underrepresented groups (into professional fields in particular), and expand into fields of burgeoning technology. These pressures to expand commitments at a time of constraints on appropriations present university management with conflicts of historically significant dimensions.

One natural reaction to this situation is to require those who are responsible for the delivery of education to increase their effort. "Faculty workload is becoming a significant issue as universities and colleges try to do more with less" (Austin and Gamson 1983, p. 23). The push for higher workloads and productivity is accomplished by drastic effects on faculty salaries, just as institutional resources as a whole have been reduced. While faculty salaries in the 1950s and 1960s outpaced the cost of living by about 65 percent (Bowen 1978), in the last decade they have dropped below the Consumer Price Index (Carnegie Council 1980). More important, faculty salaries have dropped below those for professionals in comparable jobs outside academe (Carnegie Council 1980).

Existing data suggest that faculty institutional salaries alone do not accurately reflect faculty income, because faculty earn additional income from many other sources (Dillon and Marsh 1981; Linnell 1982). It is just this fact that creates the first major conflict for the future, however. Reductions in real earnings from the institution caused by reductions in institutional resources create a climate that encourages faculty to pursue outside income just to maintain their income. Outside consulting, however, reduces faculty presence on campus and may affect productivity (Shulman 1981). Meanwhile, institutions are increasing workloads and expecting more contact between faculty and students. Thus, an institution's financial pinch creates a possible conflict with faculty rights.

Full-time Work, Effort Reporting, and Outside Consulting
Institutions are under substantial pressure to increase faculty workloads—to do more with less. Just as institutions are validly concerned with getting full-time effort, so too are state and federal agencies that support faculty salaries concerned about institutional and faculty productivity and performance. "State legislatures are major consumers of faculty workload information. They find that formulas such as student credit hours/full-time equivalents (SCH/FTE) provide a manageable approach to understanding how faculty responsibilities fit into campus management issues" (Shulman 1980a, p. 6). As finances decline, such measurement tools will have even more meaning to external state agencies for allocation and for internal decision making (Henard 1979; Huther 1974; Millett 1984).

While many researchers have investigated methodologies for measuring institutional and faculty productivity (Bowen 1974; Doi 1974; Folger 1977; Wallhaus 1975), the impetus for doing so has shifted from the desire to know to the necessity to use the information for decision making.

Perhaps the biggest change that has occurred is in the intentions behind the collection of faculty workload data—the purposes for which the data are to be used. The main trend here is that recent financial stresses on institutions of higher education have created great concern for increased efficiency in institutional operations, with faculty load data needed for unit cost studies, program budgeting, planning, and cost benefit analyses. The entry of collective bargaining into academic staffing of higher education may give further emphasis to faculty workload definition and measurement for purposes of equity and for uniformity (Stecklein 1974, pp. 1–2).

The desire to use these data on workload to justify expenditures and costs is exemplified in the promulgation of the Office of Management and Budget's Circular A-21, "Cost Principles for Educational Universities." The regulations dictate the manner in which universities are to determine the costs attributable to federal grants and contracts. "The cost of a sponsored agreement is comprised of the allowable direct costs incident to its performance, plus the allocable portion of allowable indirect costs of the institution" (p. 12370). To determine what portion of faculty salaries is allocable to federally sponsored projects, the regulations require institutions to collect data on 100 percent of the faculty member's activity. In this way, the federal government ensures against institutions being paid twice for the same effort.

Institutions are given the option of using one of two different payroll distribution formulas to collect the justifying data: "personal activity reporting systems" or the "monitored workload system." In either case, the government shifts the burden to the university's "payroll distribution system to identify all committed cost sharing effort" (Binkley 1979, p. 17).

Reaction by the academic community to the federal requirement that all faculty, whether or not involved in sponsored research, report workload in detail was strong (Association of American Universities 1980; Shulman 1980a). Although the federal government recognized the inherent difficulties in gathering such data "with a high degree of precision" and accepts "reasonably accurate approximations," the requirement to report nonetheless remains. Institutions must certify the accuracy of their reports, and to do so meaningfully requires faculty members' cooperation and honesty.

Requiring faculty to report their full-time, institutionally related efforts highlights the need to define "full-time effort." Many collective bargaining contracts define such effort but mostly in terms of contact hours (Mortimer and Lozier 1974b). What remains undefined is precisely how much time faculty actually spend on campus performing institutional duties and the question of whether faculty should be allowed to earn money off campus regardless of the time spent on campus. Thus, reporting internal effort raises questions about faculty rights to consult off campus.

There is evidence of legislative concern about activities that supplement faculty income or involve time that appears already to be salaried and thus belongs to the institution. Increased governmental attention to time accountability, reflected in such university requirements as "monitored workloads" and "personnel activity re-

*ports" for funded research projects, reflects suspicion
that outside activities drain off significant amounts of
faculty time. It may be that this time should be devoted
to research projects for which faculty are paid out of
public monies. In the past, it was generally assumed that
faculty time was devoted primarily to university responsibilities including funded research; this assumption is
now being seriously questioned* (Linnell 1982, p. 24).

Further, information about faculty workload, once col-
lected, will be consumed internally. Some faculty will use
it to dramatize disparities in courseloads between disciplines, just as comparisons of salary between disciplines
have resulted in recent litigation [*Spaulding* v. *University
of Washington*, 740 F.2d 686 (9th Cir. 1984)].

All these factors highlight a concern for how colleges
and universities will treat faculty in their work assignments. Faculty have traditionally been free to determine
what they teach and how they go about it (Austin and
Gamson 1983, p. 30), subject to the classroom load assignment, which itself is often collegially determined. Faculty
obligations to work full time, as that term literally implies,
potentially infringe upon the freedom of faculty to serve
the community, whether or not for additional pay.

Relations with the Private Sector and Conflicts of Interest
American institutions of higher education have long been
averse to a strong service relationship with industry (Bok
1982, pp. 61–89). But academics' attitudes have varied
toward the social obligation of higher education to the
broader community:

*One needs very little imagination to envisage teams of
teachers upgrading inner-city schools, physical education and theatre and dance personnel designing programs suited to spaces with little grass, sociologist-
psychologist teams creating new, more compassionate
ways to enforce laws, biologists inventing easy-to-use
methods of doing away with rodents, and home econo-
mists creating inexpensive accouterments for home dec-
orating. Why aren't these things being done now? Perhaps because the university places little value on this*

kind of activity and thus chooses not to reward, much less encourage, this type of effort (Johnson 1968, p. 423).

More recently, institutions of higher education have overcome traditional fears and are entering into relationships with industry, particularly in bioengineering. The relationships benefit both organizations—the industry through the application of great minds to productive applied research and the university through the influx of substantial monies and modern equipment (Crosson 1983, p. 73).

There are several strong motivations for academic institutions and their faculties to seek industry support for research. First, there is genuine interest in facilitating the transfer of technology—from discovery to use—to contribute to the health and productivity of society; second, there is interest in ongoing dialogue between academic and industry which could improve the level of applied science by close association with industry applications; and, third, academic institutions and their faculty members are feeling particularly hard-pressed financially and see such cooperation with industry as a way of compensating for a small but important part of the support lost from federal sources (Statement 1982).

Just as state and federal governments are imposing reporting requirements on institutions to ensure they are managed well, however, so too will industry expect that institutions be fully accountable to it. Industries will require not only time-effort reporting but also reporting of inventions, nonpatentable discoveries, and content of exploratory research to determine the potential for application —which is a logical exchange for the funds they provide and for the accountability those organizations have to their stockholders (Fowler 1982–83).

This profit motive for research has not been motivated only by outside industry. Higher education institutions themselves lobbied hard and long to secure patent rights previously held by the federal government to inventions discovered under federal grants by their faculties. The Patent and Trademark Amendment of 1980 grants to institutions the right to patent and market faculty inventions and keep the royalties. With this governmental largess, however, again come certain requirements for reporting (Lachs 1983–84, pp. 276–79).

Thus, institutions are forging cooperative ventures with industry and using outside research foundations to market patents in competition with industry (Daniels et al. 1977). Individual faculty are forming their own companies and offering stock to their institutions in exchange for the continued relationship. While most institutions have avoided these relationships because the internal regulatory prerequisites are too cumbersome to develop and they are not "well equipped" to even perform them (Bok 1982, pp. 165–68), they raise issues of universities' spawning industrial competition that may, in the long run, not be to the institutions' benefit (Noble and Pfund 1980).

The private sector already increasingly complains that faculty, instead of working as institutional employees full time, are instead working as outside professionals in competition with them. This outside faculty consultation often results in loss of opportunities for the private sector. Furthermore, private industry is viewing this competition as *subsidized* competition; that is, state or institutional monies (in the form of office space, laboratory space, equipment, and supplies) are being used to support faculty for additional income. These matters raise questions of conflicts of interest: Are faculty using their positions with academic employers to personally benefit only their own pocketbooks? Isn't this service supposed to be part of their normal university obligations? Complaints of this nature result in the promulgation of institutional rules and even closer monitoring of faculty conduct.

Summary

Many divergent factors converge upon institutions to be accountable for faculty members' performance. The financial constraints most recently experienced by American academic institutions have forced institutions to do more with less, requiring institutions first to understand how faculty spend their time and then to regulate more exactly the assignments of workload. Institutions must be able to quantify faculty time so that they can account to legislatures and other funding agents for the monies they expend.

The reporting structures established by the federal government, and used by states, have required institutions to gather data on 100 percent of faculty effort. These data are then usable to justify cost assignments for computing direct and indirect costs on federal grants and contracts. Reporting is not limited to those faculty supported by federal grants; it is required of all faculty.

Governments are not the only organizations requiring justification for monies invested in higher education. Private industry, entering cooperative relationships with universities in greater numbers to foster proprietary research, expects institutions to account for the monies contributed. Futhermore, industry expects the enterprise to be managed in a business-like manner.

All these external pressures to account for faculty actions and workload are compounded by internal forces that use this information for their own purposes. Disciplinary differences in workload and salary are highlighted, and pressures to equalize treatment deepen. The upsurge of faculty collective bargaining is a prime example of faculties' using negotiated agreements to regulate working conditions.

Ultimately, these pressures for accountability for and regulation of faculty conduct and workload compound, and their combined impact can suffocate an institution (Carnegie Foundation 1982; Hobbs 1978). Moreover, their impact falls squarely on the shoulders of the faculty themselves. It is they who must complete the forms and account for their time and effort—an intrusion into their traditional autonomy. This intrusion comes at a time when faculty already feel the squeeze of relative salary depression and as a result are increasing their external consulting, further exacerbating funding agencies' and private industries' concerns about faculty work time. This widening cycle of accountability and responsibility on the part of institutions has been alleged to smack squarely into the concept of academic freedom and to infringe upon the traditional independence that faculty have possessed. Nonetheless, institutions are actively promulgating rules to define more specifically the terms of the faculty employment contract, violations of which can result in dismissal. It thus becomes essential to examine some of these new restrictions and the manner in which they interrelate and conflict with traditional academic freedoms.

Freedom in research is fundamental to the advancement of truth. Academic freedom in its teaching aspect is fundamental for the protection of the rights of the teacher in teaching and of the student to freedom in learning (AAUP 1977a, p. 2).

Academic freedom is the right faculty possess to search out new and controversial topics and to express them freely. Tenure was created to protect that freedom (Metzger 1979). Tenure systems ensure that professors who have successfully passed their probationary status will not be removed from their positions except for stated and proven reasons. "Although academic tenure does not constitute a guarantee of life employment, i.e., tenured teachers may be released for 'cause'. . . , it denotes clearly defined limitations upon the institution's power to terminate the teachers' services" [*AAUP* v. *Bloomfield College*, 129 N.J. Super. 249, 322 A.2d 846 (1974), pp. 263, 853]. Such causes are for institutions to determine in their tenure contracts, because it is the institution that establishes the contract— or in public institutions, the property rights bestowed by tenure on faculty [*Board of Regents* v. *Roth*, 408 U.S. 564 (1972)]. Where not so defined, the historically accepted causes discussed earlier are often incorporated into the tenure contract by the courts. Cause cannot include punishment for the exercise by faculty of academic freedom in teaching and research, however. "The idea of academic freedom [is] that a teacher or professor is free to teach or profess, without interference, in any and all aspects of that course or subject . . ." (Bornheimer, Burns, and Dunke 1973, p. 18).

Academic freedom is the right faculty possess to search out new and controversial topics and to express them freely.

Certain forces, however, restrict institutional tolerance of certain conduct by faculty. So long as this conduct is not protected by tenure as infringing upon academic freedom, it may become valid cause for discipline or dismissal. But defining what comes under academic freedom is sometimes difficult, as is knowing how much control a college can exercise over the conduct of faculty in the performance of their jobs without impinging on that particular right.

It thus becomes necessary to explore some of these emerging areas to determine what conduct institutions can proscribe and what faculty conduct may not be limited.

Faculty Full-time Performance

Full-time faculty owe their institutions 100 percent of their effort. This amount may not correspond to 100 percent of their working time, however. The concept of what constitutes full-time service for a faculty member has never been well understood or defined. Faculty have long felt that they have the unlimited authority to schedule their time, subject only to meeting their classes. Thus, it is common for faculty to be away from the office or even off campus. Although they spend, on average, more than an equivalent amount of hours performing university functions, faculty have never felt compelled to be "on duty" the traditional 40-hour work week expected of secretarial and other institutional support staff. This unique characteristic of independence should by no means be interpreted to include the right not to work at all or the right to do only those things for which specific hourly commitments have been made. The institution, the state, and the federal agencies that support the efforts of faculty are entitled to get full-time effort for full-time salary.

What is full-time faculty effort? Faculty work, on the average, 44 to 55 hours a week during the academic calendar (Ladd 1979; Romney 1971; Yuker 1974). Within this work week, teaching encompasses the majority of time, though the percentage varies with type of institution (Baldridge et al. 1978), with faculty age (Thompson 1971), and discipline (Jedamus 1974). Faculty at research universities spend less time in the classroom than faculty at other types of institutions (Fulton and Trow 1974). Indeed, faculty at two-year institutions spend 70 percent of their faculty time in teaching-related duties, while faculty at research universities spend considerably less, at 33 percent (Shulman 1980a). Others have found different percentages, but the spread between institutions remains (Ladd and Lipset 1977; Willie and Stecklein 1981).

Particularly at elite institutions, the balance of faculty time is presumably spent in research, publication, service, and administration (Baldridge et al. 1978; Ladd 1979; Ladd and Lipset 1977; Rich and Jolicoeur 1978). Nearly 90 percent of all faculty also spend time earning some form of supplemental income, however (Ladd and Lipset 1977). Outside consulting, private practice, and other nonuniversity, duty-oriented conduct are the predominant sources of supplemental income (Linnell 1982; Marsh and Dillon 1980).

While faculty have admittedly lost purchasing power over the last decade, institutions are nevertheless entitled to expect to receive full-time work for full-time pay. Faculty time, therefore, may be regulated to ensure that they are performing required institutional services and are not neglecting their institutional responsibilities to provide services for which additional outside remuneration is received. This situation is especially true in public institutions, where legislators view faculty members' outside consulting as a form of double dipping (Jolly 1978). The questions become how much outside activity is permissible and whether the limitations that institutions prescribe interfere with faculty freedoms.

Regulation of outside consulting

In 1978, a task force sponsored by the Association of American Universities, American Council on Education, and National Association of State Universities and Land-Grant Colleges developed *Principles to Govern College and University Compensation Policies*. The statement was designed to provide guidance for institutional policies and practices governing the compensation of faculty engaged in government-sponsored research. In reference to outside practice by faculty, the statement provides:

> *In the interest of all concerned, universities and colleges should establish and disseminate to faculty and administrators explicit compensation policies and practices that incorporate the following:*
>
> *1. A policy on consulting that clearly states a maximum allowed time for such activity and the responsibility of individuals*
>
>> *(a) to comply with institutional compensation policies,*
>>
>> *(b) to conform with professional standards of ethical conduct,*
>>
>> *(c) to inform and confer with appropriate institutional officers on the nature and extent of consulting that could impair or conflict with the individual's primary responsibilities to the university or college, and*

(d) *to inform and confer with appropriate institutional officers on the nature and extent of consulting that could impair or conflict with the individual's or institution's responsibilities to granting agencies, with the expectation that university and college officers will provide granting agencies proper notice.*
2. *A policy for the summer and other recess periods.*
3. *A policy to prevent double payment for the same duty.*
4. *Institutional monitoring to ensure consistent implementation of these principles within each unit of the college or university* (pp. 1–2).

A specific policy is important in regulating the activities of faculty, whether in state or privately funded institutions, particularly with the present emphasis on accountability. In a survey of research and doctoral-granting universities, a majority of respondent institutions indicated that their universities had policies on faculty consulting (Dillon and Bane 1980). This finding was consistent with an earlier survey, which also showed that a majority of the responding institutions had formal policies regarding consulting, private practice, and other compensated activities (Rich and Brown 1976). The most common limitation on outside consulting was one day per seven-day week, with the requirement of obtaining prior approval for such activity from the appropriate dean or vice president. Other policies included no limitations, limitations by hours or days per specified length of work week, or limitations specified by percentage of the academic year or in terms of salary (Dillon and Bane 1980).

In some fields, significant percentages of faculty are part time. Policies that limit outside practice often are made to apply to such part-time faculty as well. Stanford University's policy on outside consulting and practice, which limits full-time faculty to 13 days (one day per calendar week) outside consulting per quarter, has incorporated within it a formula for determining limitations on outside consulting for part-time faculty (Stanford University 1977). The limit for full-time faculty is prorated for part-time faculty as follows:

$13 \times F + (1 - F) \times 6 \times 13$

F being the fraction of full-time duty

13 representing the average number of weeks per quarter

6 representing the maximum number of days per week
. . . likely to be devoted to professional activities
(Stanford University 1977).

The issues of whether the university has the authority to limit outside faculty work and whether such limitations infringe upon faculty freedoms were squarely faced by the courts in *Gross* v. *University of Tennessee* [448 F. Supp. 245 (W.D. Tenn. 1978), *aff'd*, 620 F.2d 109 (6th Cir. 1980)]. The institution had a longstanding requirement that faculty annually execute an agreement limiting their external income. The express purpose was to ensure that full-time faculty devote maximum effort to their teaching and research. Two tenured professors, one of whom was also a department chair in the university's Health Sciences Center, refused to execute the agreement, although, the court noted, they had signed the agreements in the years before receiving tenure. They were dismissed for failure to abide by university rules in violation of their contract and appointments.

The court found, in a suit for reinstatement instituted by the faculty members, that the institutional requirement was valid and that a violation of the professors' due process rights to engage in unlimited private practice of medicine did not exist:

> *Bearing in mind that federal courts are to play an extremely limited role in reviewing the merits of personnel decisions made by public agencies, the Court holds that plaintiffs have no constitutional right to engage in the unlimited private practice of medicine while holding a public position of employment. The Court further holds that the income limiting agreements utilized were rationally related to the espoused legitimate goals of fostering full-time devotion to teaching duties. The termination of plaintiffs by defendants for their refusal to sign the agreements infringed no constitutionally protected right of plaintiffs* (448 F. Supp., p. 248).

The principles of this case apply to private and to public institutions of higher learning [*Wood* v. *University of Tulsa* (Ct. App. Okla. No. 53,230, March 17, 1981)].

Internal controls on faculty workload and insubordination
While institutions apparently have the authority to regulate the extent of outside work, they do not have the general authority to regulate the type of outside work. Within the institution, however, controls over the content areas of work are being exerted, particularly when institutional finances have been reduced and faculty efforts and workloads are being redirected as a result. Such financial pressures have broadened institutional exercises of authority over faculty members' work.

It is apparent that higher education today is a buyer's market and that faculty employment is being curtailed.

> *Fewer faculty will achieve tenure. Many will be hired on nontenure tracks; others will be denied tenure because of the already high percentage of tenured faculty on campus. . . . Given decreased mobility and rewards, it is likely that those faculty will remain in education at their institutions for another 20 to 30 years. Therefore, by and large, most colleges already have the faculty with whom they will enter the twenty-first century* (Brooks and German 1983, pp. 33–34).

With fewer replacements being hired and existing faculty having to cover wider areas, the tendency increases for assignments to teach in areas not of one's personal choice. Thus, fiscal restraints will impinge upon the traditional faculty freedoms of what to teach and what to research.

Courts have generally favored institutions' authority to require faculty to perform their internally assigned tasks, even if the tasks are not of the faculty member's choosing. The prerogative to assign specific work is one of several managerial prerogatives outweighing many faculty freedoms.

> *Thus, certain legitimate state interests may limit the right of a public employee, specifically the right of a state university professor, to say and do what he pleases: for example (1) the need to maintain discipline*

and harmony among co-workers; (2) the need for confi-
dentiality; (3) the need to curtail conduct which impedes
the teacher's proper and competent performance of his
daily duties; (4) the need to encourage a close and per-
sonal relationship between the employees and his superi-
ors, when that relationship calls for loyalty and confi-
dence; (5) the need to maintain a competition of
different views in the classroom and to prevent the use
of the classroom by a teacher deliberately to proselytize
for a certain cause or knowingly to emphasize only that
selection of data best conforming to his own personal
biases; (6) the need to prevent activities disruptive of the
educational process and to provide for the orderly func-
tioning of the university [*Keddie* v. *Pennsylvania State*
University, 412 F. Supp. 1264 (M.D. Pa. 1976), p. 1271].

In *Stastny* v. *Board of Trustees,* a tenured professor of
history defied institutional directives to be present for reg-
istration and the opening of classes. Instead, he took an
unauthorized leave of absence to present a scholarly paper
at a foreign conference. The professor was dismissed for
insubordination but asserted in court that his defiance was
"merely a single respectful act of disobedience," not of
insubordination, and that his dismissal violated his right to
academic freedom and freedom of expression (p. 502). The
court rejected these arguments, observing that "academic
freedom is not a license for activity at variance with job-
related procedures and requirements, nor does it encompass activities which are internally destructive to the
proper function of the university or disruptive to the education process" (p. 504). It is the institution that defines
what is in conformance with the education process.

One tenured faculty member's failure to complete work
and reports required for projects under contract by the
university and to observe and follow university rules and
procedures in the accounting for and expenditure of funds
and purchase of equipment also justified termination for
cause. In *Bates* v. *Sponberg* [547 F.2d 325 (6th Cir. 1976)],
the faculty member was provided appropriate administrative hearings before the faculty grievance committee. The
committee found that his actions, which he asserted were a
form of protest against the university's accounting procedures, were unjustified. The committee unanimously sup-

ported his termination, which was affirmed by the president, the board of regents, and ultimately the courts.

Conflicts over the regulation of faculty academic assignments and the imposition of reporting requirements have been resolved in favor of the institution. Provided the regulations or assignments are reasonable and are not applied as a pretext to infringe upon faculty academic speech, no violation of academic freedom has been deemed to occur.

Faculty Pedagogy, Student Interactions, and Sexual Harassment

The manner in which faculty members teach their students has always been an area central to academic freedom. Faculty academic freedom has centered on conduct of pedagogical techniques and course content—provided the course content is relevant to the course. While failure to teach a course assigned by the institution has been held to be valid grounds for discipline and not protected by academic freedom [*Shaw* v. *Board of Trustees of Frederick Community College*, 549 F.2d 929 (4th Cir. 1976)], just as incompetence in teaching has been valid grounds for dismissal (*Chung* v. *Park* 1975), direct action that impacts instructional methodology has been viewed as an infringement of academic freedom.

The conflict arises when the faculty member teaching methodology crosses the threshold of prohibited conduct and violates students' rights to be free of sexual harassment. The faculty member in an anatomy class who uses the picture from *Playboy* to describe the female torso is simultaneously exercising his or her academic freedom in the selection of his pedagogical tools and making it uncomfortable for women students in the classroom. Such exercises of academic freedom may, under the law, have to be subservient to the concomitant rights of students to be in an educational environment free from sexual harassment.

According to the Equal Employment Opportunity Commission's guidelines on sex discrimination, sexual harassment is:

> *Unwelcome sexual advances, requests for sexual favors, or other verbal or physical conduct of a sexual nature . . . when 1) submission to such conduct is made either implicitly or explicitly a term or condition of an individ-*

ual's employment, 2) submission to or rejection of such conduct by an individual is used as the basis for employment decisions affecting such individual, or 3) such conduct has the purpose or effect of unreasonably interfering with an individual's work performance or creating an intimidating, hostile, or offensive working environment (29 CFR 1604.11).

Under this federal definition, viewed as applicable to protect students under Title IX as it is to protect faculty under Title VII [*Alexander* v. *Yale University,* 631 F.2d 178 (2d Cir. 1980)], institutions are prohibited from creating an intimidating or offensive educational environment. Clearly, certain instructional techniques are offensive to students and must be prevented. The institution is responsible for adopting grievance procedures "providing for the prompt and equitable resolution of student complaints" within the prohibitions of the act [34 CFR 106.8(b)].

In addition to the implications for instructional methodology, institutional attempts to prevent sexual harassment have also been viewed as restricting faculty members' freedom of association rights. Tales of faculty members' predicating good grades on students' sexual favors are not new to academe, but what *is* new are the actions institutions have taken to discourage, and even to punish, such unethical faculty conduct. The University of Minnesota, for example, has adopted a policy that "consenting romantic and sexual relationships between faculty and students, or between supervisor and employee, while not expressly forbidden, are generally deemed very unwise" (*Chronicle* 1984). Other institutions, concerned about the inherent imbalances of power between professors and students, have attempted to address the problem in more informal ways, including the creation of joint student/faculty committees to study the problem, student support groups, and other strategies (Perry 1983). The AAUP drafted suggested policy guidelines to help institutions respond to students' complaints about sexual harassment; a separate policy statement was necessary because the association's statement on professional ethics, although forbidding exploitation of students, was too general to be useful in dealing with harassment (Perry 1983, p. 22). The problem is a serious one from the institution's perspective, not only because of the moral issues involved but also because of the legal liability of colleges and universities found to have explicitly or implicitly permitted sexual harassment (Somers 1982). Again, it appears that faculty freedoms to interact with students must be limited, not only to comport with the canons of professional ethics but also to comply with the law.

Some authors believe the problem of sexual harassment in higher education is one of "epidemic proportion" (Dzeich and Weiner 1984, p. 15). In its most blatant stages—rape or academic punishment for refusal to consent to sexual propositions—it clearly falls within the purview of immorality (Lovain 1983–84, p. 425). When it is more indirect (through teaching techniques), though nonetheless damaging to students' education, it confronts the issue of faculty choice of teaching techniques. Whether the issue is perceived imbalances of power or more serious violations of civil or criminal laws, however, institutions' responsibility to limit faculty prerogatives in interacting with students is becoming evident on a growing number of campuses.

Scientific Misconduct

Despite the comparatively lower salaries associated with higher education, people still choose the professoriate as a career (Meléndez and de Guzmán 1983). Junior faculty have greater workloads than their senior peers, partly as a result of their having less control over their assignments and partly as a result of their needing to prove themselves to achieve tenure. Thus, their efforts are focused more on internal productivity than on outside activities (Linnell 1982).

In a large number of universities, this pressure to be more productive usually means to do research. This "intense pressure to publish, not only to obtain research grant renewals but in order to qualify for tenure" can result in violations of principles of ethics in research (Broad 1981, p. 137). The same pressures apply to all faculty in institutions driven by considerations of merit.

The scholar works within an environment that has been developed for conducting, supporting, and evaluating

*scholarly research in the single-minded pursuit of truth.
Our system, however, keeps all scholars, be they young
investigators or established figures in the field, under
considerable pressure. For those for whom the competitive pressure proves to be too great, this system can lead
to intellectual rashness and lack of rigor and, occasionally, even to academic fraud* (Yale University 1983).

Scientific misconduct is falsification of true discovery,
theft of another's discoveries, or the violation of accepted
scientific procedures in making discoveries. The Association of American Universities (AAU) has classified scientific misconduct into four broad categories: falsification of
data, plagiarism, abuse of confidentiality, and deliberate
violation of regulations applicable to research (1983, p. 1).

Falsification of data is sometimes called research fraud;
it "ranges from sheer fabrication through selective reporting, including the omission of conflicting data" (p. 1). Fab-
ricating data or changing actual data to achieve a desired
outcome is the most obvious example of such fraud, as
well as the most serious, because the reporting of false or
fictionalized research findings, particularly in the medical
field, could result in clinical applications "directly dangerous to humans" (p. 1).

Plagiarism, or the taking of another's written work and
claiming it as one's own, is the most commonly recognized
form of scientific misconduct. Other forms of plagiarism
are less easily recognized. For instance, taking credit (or
first authorship) for a graduate student's research is no less
plagiarism than failure to attribute passages from published
work. This situation is becoming a more obvious problem,
as evidenced by the recent guidelines issued by the American Psychological Association on authorship claims (Webb
1983). The AAU report includes "inadequate citation and
parsimony in referencing submission of the same data in
more than one publication by the same author" in the category of plagiarism (1983, p. 1).

Abuse of confidentiality is the misconduct most difficult
to detect. The collegial nature of academic work empha-
sizes reliance on peers' input and peers' review of research
in its formative or draft stages. When one learns of another's research ideas, methods of collecting data, or new

*Institutions'
responsibility
to limit faculty
prerogatives in
interactions
with students
is becoming
evident on a
growing
number of
campuses.*

formula and appropriates them for oneself, such conduct constitutes theft of the thought process and an "abuse" of the confidentiality on which scientific progress relies.
Abuse of confidentiality is less easy to detect than plagiarism, because no published articles or papers may be available against which the pilfered work can be compared. It is based on the same principle of "appropriation of another's work" as is plagiarism, however.

Deliberate violations of regulations applicable to research constitute a different kind of scientific misconduct. Federal regulations exist to protect human and animal subjects and to control research involving certain biomedical compounds, DNA in particular [see 45 CFR §46.101–.409 (1983); The Animal Welfare Act of 1970, 7 U.S.C. §2131 (1982), 9 CFR §2.1 (1983); and Guidelines for Research Involving Recombinant DNA Molecules, 48 Fed. Reg. 24556 (1983)]. Deliberate failure to comply with these research procedures and limitations "undermines the integrity of the research process" (AAU 1983, p. 2) and may impose substantial liability on the researcher and the researcher's institution [45 CFR §76 (1983)].

Thus, because the institution's reputation is at stake and because legal liability attaches to the failure by faculty to conform to stated research procedures, institutions are compelled to impose restrictions on faculty freedoms to use certain research protocols (Mishkin 1983) and to promulgate procedures to ensure compliance with those processes and investigate allegations of their breach (Olswang and Lee 1984). Do such stipulations, however, unjustly infringe on faculty academic freedom?

Academic freedom protects faculty from being dismissed or otherwise having their contract rights—tenure—impaired for unpopular thought, publication, research, or speech. Scientific misconduct is the exact opposite of this freedom, antithetical to it, and strikes at the heart of the scientific enterprise (AAU 1983, p. 1). In fact, the AAUP's 1940 statement asserts that "freedom in research is fundamental to the advancement of truth" (1977a, p. 2), suggesting that freedom in research is not separable from truth. A later AAUP statement asserts that a faculty member's "primary responsibility to his subject is to seek and to state the truth . . . , practic[ing] intellectual honesty" (1977e, p. 65).

Thus, while conduct in research is regulated to a greater extent, following peer-developed protocols for research does not unduly restrict academic freedom.

Ownership of Faculty Products: Patents and Copyrights
For many years, colleges and universities have taken the position that the product of a faculty member's labor belonged to the faculty member. Many institutions thus chose not to adopt institutional policies on patents or copyrights. Further, many believed that profit-making ventures were inimical to the purposes of higher education (Palmer 1974): The purpose of higher education was the creation and free development of knowledge; therefore, the patenting process might inhibit that dissemination of knowledge. The two processes did not mix in higher education (Lachs 1983–84, p. 264).

With increasing frequency, institutions have begun to change their views and to actively assert their ownership claims over faculty inventions and creations. Employers are entitled to assert rights over patentable inventions based on the principle that the work performed by the employee is owned by the employer. The assertion of this claim is generally incorporated into the employment contract. Thus, as a condition of employment, faculty are obligated to disclose to the university all inventions that may be patented.

Because patents—the right to exclude others from use of the invention for a period of 17 years in exchange for the full disclosure of the invention's elements to the public through the patent office—have value, institutions will now more actively enforce their ownership rights. This situation is exemplified by the promulgation of the Patent and Trademarks Amendments of 1980 (P.L. 96–517), which awards universities the right to patents developed by faculty under federal grants and contracts and obligates those institutions to license the patents or forfeit the rights back to the government (Smith 1981–82).

This impetus to acquire and market faculty inventions inhibits normal faculty prerogatives of academic freedom in several ways. First, it restricts the faculty member's ability to acquire property rights in his or her intellectual products. Further, it potentially punishes them for quick publication of their research findings, for the publication of research before a patent application is filed results in the loss of that patent to the public domain. Institutional ownership of patent and copyright rights also puts faculty in jeopardy of violating their employment and/or tenure contract should they decide to publish research results of a patentable nature. (Only actual publication of research results in the loss of patent rights; mere submission of an article for peer review is not deemed to be a publication and thus does not result in the loss of patent rights [*Application of Schlitter*, 234 F.2d 882 (C.C.P.A. 1956)].)

The assertion of patent rights over faculty inventions has spread to the assertion of copyright rights, with courts holding that certain computer programs are not patentable but instead must be copyrighted to be protected [*Diamond* v. *Diehr*, 450 U.S. 175 (1981); *Gottschalk* v. *Benson*, 409 U.S. 63 (1972)]. Furthermore, the Copyright Act itself was amended in 1980 to explicitly include computer programs (17 U.S.C. 101).

Institutions have historically behaved as though the writings of faculty were the property of the authors. Even if a textbook results, virtually no institution has asserted ownership rights over faculty-produced scholarship. But computer programs, or instructional media, or concert tapes, are no less scholarly works for the mathematician, history professor, or music instructor than is the book for the English professor. Thus, the assertion of rights in some areas has the potential for infringing upon faculty rights in others.

The danger also exists "of turning university investigators from basic research projects to short-term goals which promise immediate commercial rewards" (Lachs 1983–84, p. 265). This corruption of the academic ethic of the search for truth, rather than "engaging in research of little intrinsic interest just to obtain patentable inventions," is the most serious argument against university patent policies. Further, by making patenting profitable—rather than rewarding academic discovery per se—secrecy and intense rivalries can develop, to the detriment of collegiality (Lachs 1983–84, p. 270). Institutions should attempt to balance their active encouragement of patents with a concern for the possible result of prostituting intellectual discovery for profit.

Perhaps the most visible threat to academic freedom comes, however, from the ever-increasing relationships between industry and educational institutions. While guidelines exist to control even the most simple of research/industry relationships (Fowler 1982–83), it must be accepted that "the appropriate development of new opportunities in academic/industrial relations presents universities with a host of problems. The most important of these is the potential distortion such relationships may cause to academic objectives" (Statement 1982, p. 2).

Conflicts of Interest
Many of the aforementioned issues also could fall within the scope of conflict of interest. Consulting relationships by faculty with outside businesses "create the potential for loss of open and free inquiry on campus. . . . Some faculty may have signed consulting agreements with external companies which are in conflict with their obligations to their own institutions or with contractual agreements between the institution and research sponsors" (Linnell 1982, p. 61).

Conflicts of interest occur in a myriad of forms. Many state laws define conflicts of interest for public employees in terms of prohibiting the use of one's state position for personal economic benefit (Alexander 1980, pp. 132–33). Put another way, a faculty member may not receive something extra of personal benefit, or for the benefit of one of his or her relations, if the performance of the task is expected of the faculty in the normal course of duties for his or her remunerated job.

The conflict most dangerous to academic freedom is that touching the ethics of the profession (Dillon 1979; Shulman 1980b). "Intellectual conflicts may be less obvious but they are at the heart of the academic enterprise. Cognitive dissonance—the subtle shifting of one's ideas toward those positions favoring personal interests—can occur in the best of minds" (Linnell 1982, p. 62).

Tales of faculty members leaving the university and striking it rich with new inventions are rampant (Lachs 1983–84, p. 290). Such developments "underscore the need for universities to consider the rules and procedures necessary to ensure that faculty members fulfill their responsibilities to teaching and research, and to avoid conflicts of interest" (Statement 1982, p. 6).

Currently, institutional attempts to limit the outside activities of faculty rely more on voluntary cooperation than on formal enforcement of the rules, but the magnitude of the problem facing academe in this regard is just beginning to become evident. The University of California, as an example, has gone beyond voluntary cooperation and has implemented regulations that attempt to prevent private corporate sponsors from restricting the publication of research findings or skewing the type of research conducted. The university terminated the research contracts of three faculty members in mid-1983; two of the faculty members were members of the funding agent's board of directors and had received consulting fees from the company, and the third had agreed to suppress publication of his research findings for two years (Sanger 1983).

The balance between careful enforcement of university regulations and academic freedom is often difficult to maintain, especially in light of the additional power and emoluments that faculty with substantial outside funding enjoy. The institution's interest in preserving its own independence from corporate influence, however, and the need to protect the freedom of its faculty to conduct research relatively free of external pressure for certain results, high profits, or secrecy suggest that institutional enforcement of explicit regulations against conflicts of interest will enhance, rather than inhibit, faculty academic freedom (Bouton 1983). To do less, however, would potentially sacrifice the integrity of those faculty who respect the separation of institutional obligations and personal pecuniary motivations (Dill 1982; Schurr 1982).

Summary
Controls over faculty conduct are increasing. They are generated from a myriad of external and internal forces requiring faculty to account for their time and their extramural and intramural activities. Many of these emerging limitations, while building over years, have been energetically activated by the recent declines in the financial resources available to colleges and universities.

At the heart of the wave of demands for limitations on faculty conduct is the apparent failure of external organizations to comprehend what faculty jobs entail. What full-time performance means has not been clearly described. Thus, the perception that faculty do not spend full-time effort earning their full-time salary is difficult to verify or refute.

This perception is compounded by several factors. First, some legislators see faculty consulting as double dipping; the private sector sees it as state-subsidized competition. The burgeoning potential of patents and copyrights to generate profit requires institutions to negotiate with sponsors and to enact controls that protect the respective investments of faculty, sponsors, and universities in products whose potential may be totally unforeseen. Finally, new social concerns for the treatment of women and for disciplinary equity require new standards of conduct and vigilant but fair enforcement codes.

All these factors converge to generate more limitations on traditional faculty freedoms, usually incorporated into terms of the tenure contract. Yet each alone, while limiting in its particular way, does not necessarily infringe upon the right of speech and thought. As a whole, however, they burden the faculty and expand the "causal" definitions under which tenure can be removed.

FACULTY PERFORMANCE, ACCOUNTABILITY, AND PERIODIC REVIEW

Previous sections focused primarily on institutions' regulation of faculty time, effort, duties, and behavior. Whether spawned by governmental reporting requirements, internal concerns for efficiency and effectiveness, or in response to external complaints or opportunities, colleges and university administrators will be compelled to examine the performance of faculty more closely than ever before.

Equally—if not more—important to the future of higher education is the movement to review and examine the substantive performance of faculty, not just their objective time contribution. Simply putting in time does not promote excellence, nor does it produce good teaching or make new discoveries. Institutions, the students who contract with the university for their education, and private and public funding sources that pay to support the institution expect college administrations to provide effective teachers and researchers. Thus, pressure has increased to discipline those who do not perform.

Simply putting in time does not promote excellence, nor does it produce good teaching or make new discoveries.

The emphasis on the evaluation of faculty is not new, but it has been given additional impetus by a number of recent changes in higher education. The trend toward accountability has focused attention on the evaluation of the performance of the faculty. Students insist upon evaluation of faculty, legislators and the public believe it should be required and more rigorous, and boards of trustees and system administrators expect systematic, thorough well-developed evaluation policies (Stroup 1983, p. 47).

It is apparent that not all faculty achieve at the same rate, and some stop achieving altogether. Several authors have examined causes for decline in faculty productivity. In some cases, it may be the result of "burnout."

Burnout in academe is the result of negatively perceived work-related events or conditions that produce a level of persistent stress resulting in chronic frustration, tiredness or exhaustion, adverse behavior, and inefficiency and/or dysfunction in one's work (Meléndez and de Guzmán 1983, p. 16).

Burnout results in conflicts with authority, which many view as a source of the "disease," increased absenteeism, low morale, and incapability of functioning properly (Baldwin and Blackburn 1983; White 1980).

Whether a faculty member's performance decreases because of burnout or because he or she simply feels "stuck"—does not perform because of a lack of stimulation, desire, or challenge (Meléndez and de Guzmán 1983, p. 17)—it is an institutional problem in two ways: first, it must be identified; second, it must be remediated.

Optimally, the goal of any institutionally mandated performance review system would be to reward merit or, conversely, to identify deficiencies and to provide all necessary assistance to remedy the situation. "Good faculty personnel policies shape opportunities for individual growth and development" (Fuller 1983, p. 100). But regardless of the most altruistic goals of a review system, it will still be viewed with skepticism and fear and a threat to faculty security.

Institutional regulations requiring mandatory reviews of probationary faculty exist throughout education. Such reviews exist to determine whether probationary faculty meet scholarly and instructional standards justifying the award of tenure. And because the "granting of tenure is the mode of admission to the university association" (Jacques 1976, p. 60), evaluation of competency in the probationary stages of a faculty member's appointment is traditionally vested initially in the faculty. Placing this responsibility in the faculty is consistent with the AAUP principles (AAUP 1977d), and the courts have consistently viewed faculty as the most appropriate evaluators of academic merit (Lee *In press*).

Institutional regulations mandate faculty reviews of probationary faculty before the award of tenure, yet generally very few similar requirements exist for reviewing and evaluating the continued performance of tenured faculty to ensure they are maintaining the standards of performance that justified the initial award of tenure (Chait and Ford 1982). The 1982 National Commission on Higher Education Issues recommended the development of such systems of post-tenure review. And while the AAUP and other national organizations are studying the question of periodic performance review at the present time, tenured faculty have been generally viewed in the past as not subject to such reevaluation.

While, however, "tenure ensures against the infringement of academic freedom, it does not insulate faculty from fair assessments of their competence to perform appointed duties. Periodic reviews themselves do not violate the principles of academic freedom; they simply assess performance in order to provide information which may be used for a variety of purposes" (Olswang and Fantel 1980–81, pp. 26–27). Much has been written about the evaluative process (Centra 1979; Miller 1972; Seldin 1980; Smith 1976; Waggaman 1983) and the need to use consistent and objective criteria in making faculty personnel decisions (Gillmore 1983–84; Stroup 1983). So long as systematic processes are in place to guide the evaluations, periodic performance reviews can be instituted without violating faculty freedoms (Bennett and Chater 1984).

Outcomes from reviews alone cannot be a basis for immediate revocation of tenure. All appropriate and required mechanisms of due process must be afforded faculty if such data are to be used to demonstrate failure of performance justifying the removal of tenure.

The use of individual faculty assessments of performance has also been held valid in the selection of faculty to be removed in cases of financial exigency [*Bignall* v. *North Idaho College*, 538 F.2d 243 (9th Cir. 1976); *Krotkoff* v. *Goucher College*, 585 F.2d 675 (4th Cir. 1978); *Levitt* v. *Board of Trustees of Nebraska State College*, 376 F. Supp. 945 (D. Neb. 1974)]. But despite the legality of using faculty evaluation in cases of fiscal retrenchment, some authors have objected to the application of performance evaluation in this process.

> *It is deceptively easy to argue that retrenchment decisions should take into account the relatively superior performance of one faculty member as opposed to another. But the issue of evaluation of tenured faculty is itself controversial and probably would not survive being tied to issues of retrenchment* (Mortimer 1981, p. 168).

The call for faculty accountability in performance can be compared to similar challenges to other professionals. Like faculty who receive tenure for life, attorneys are licensed and deemed able to perform their duties throughout their lives until challenged through professional disciplinary action. Such challenges occur normally after a demonstration of incompetence by the lawyer (Oakes 1978). And, as with faculty, attorneys are reluctant to discipline their own colleagues (Marks and Cathcart 1974). Public criticism of attorneys and the profession's harboring of incompetents, however, is leading to mandatory recertification requirements in many states (Woytash 1978). Similarly, the teaching profession has lost some of its public esteem and trust, and self-regulation of performance is preferable to imposed accountability.

Of interest also is the parallel between periodic review of faculty performance and AAUP requirements for the periodic evaluation of administrators' performance.

> *The decision to retain or, more significantly, not to retain an administrator should be subject to the same deliberation process and made by the same groups responsible for his selection. Whereas the selection of an administrator is essentially an exercise of foresight, a decision respecting his retention affords the opportunity for relevant academic groups to assess, on the basis of experience, the confidence in which the administration is held* (AAUP 1977b, p. 50).

One might argue that a college's or university's interest in high-quality performance of its faculty is of no less importance than its interest in the quality of administrative performance. Periodic review of faculty performance, for both tenured and untenured faculty, is also viewed as essential to maintain public faith in the quality of the institution (Marcus, Leone, and Goldberg 1983, pp. 50–51).

Thus, the periodic review of faculty teaching, research, and service is one answer to the increasing demand that institutions ensure the maintenance of faculty competence and effort. It is one way for institutions to ensure to themselves and their supporters that the best education is being provided for the dollars expended. But such avenues of accountability present challenges to tradition, and, if implemented poorly or without faculty participation or if performed arbitrarily or unfairly, they can be used as a subterfuge to weaken faculty academic freedoms. Evaluating and ensuring the continued competence of faculty does not itself infringe on those freedoms, however, as competence is a condition to the retention of tenure.

> *Systems of post-tenure evaluation provide an excellent way to preserve the strengths of tenure while also allaying public suspicions about tenure and concerns about faculty vigor and accountability. Failure to address these increasing public concerns will inevitably increase the likelihood of external regulation* (Bennett and Chater 1984, p. 38).

CONCLUSIONS AND RECOMMENDATIONS

As a result of externally imposed regulations and the need to respond to inquiries about efficiency and effectiveness, colleges and universities are increasingly compelled to promulgate and enforce limitations in areas of traditional faculty autonomy. These limitations, which address outside consulting, conflict of interest, ownership of patents and copyrights, and the like, all become incorporated by reference into the faculty contract. As a result, these rules further confine the actions of faculty, and violations of their terms become valid cause for faculty discipline or dismissal.

The reasons that institutions must promulgate such rules vary. Some result from federal or state laws or agency regulations. Some result from internal needs to account for fees or allocations from legislatures. Some are generated in response to the need to raise as much revenue as possible in an era of shrinking resources. But whatever the reason, they have generally been considered legal and enforceable. And so long as they do not directly inhibit or infringe upon faculty freedom of speech and thought, they do not offend academic freedom.

Colleges and universities are increasingly compelled to promulgate and enforce limitations in areas of traditional faculty autonomy.

Institutional Environment

The effect of such regulations is to make higher education a less than optimal place to work. Such intrinsic factors as autonomy and freedom contribute most to faculty satisfaction (Bess 1981; Eckert and Williams 1972), but if that autonomy is challenged or restricted, the college environment becomes less enjoyable as a workplace and the quality of performance suffers (Austin and Gamson 1983; Meléndez and de Guzmán 1983).

> *Increasing numbers of academics and would-be academics no longer see a career in academe as the route to success and happiness. . . . A substantial minority of today's middle-aged academics are both interested in leaving academe and believe that they would be as happy or more happy with a career outside academe . . .* (Patton 1983, p. 43).

Thus, while increased regulation of faculty conduct may not be inconsistent with academic freedom as it has evolved, it does nonetheless seriously affect faculty job satisfaction and thus faculty morale. Assuming that institutions must to some degree impose these regulations on faculty conduct to be fully responsive to those agencies to whom they must report, the question then becomes not why the regulations were imposed, but how. The manner by which such regulations are adopted and concern for their impact on the faculty may be the answer to how best to maintain an educational environment conducive to academic freedom and faculty autonomy.

Faculty Participation, Morale, and Satisfaction
Faculty morale in general declined during the 1970s (Anderson 1983), and further decline is likely as a result of financial problems and increased regulation:

> *The problems facing higher education today are making academic life far from idyllic. Faculty are experiencing stress from a decline in extrinsic rewards and increased workloads. The strong intrinsic motivation characteristic of college faculty seems to be threatened. Pressures for more productivity come at the same time that the faculty's power in their institutions is declining* (Austin and Gamson 1983, p. 44).

Faculty involvement in all decision-making activities has declined. Faculty participation in governance structures has declined over recent years, and faculty governance structures spend their time on matters of less than critical importance (Carnegie Foundation 1982). This decline in the level of participation has affected morale. Even in times of difficult decisions, morale will be bolstered by faculty involvement (Anderson 1983; Hammond and Tompkins 1983; Rose and Hample 1981; Williams, Olswang, and Hargett *In press*). But today faculty believe that they are less involved in institutional decision making (Brooks and German 1983; Magarrell 1982).

One mechanism to offset the negative effects on faculty autonomy and job satisfaction and to address the necessary issues of accountability outlined earlier is to involve faculty directly in the study of and promulgation of regulations for professional conduct. The more faculty participate in the decisions, the more likely they will accept them

(Powers and Powers 1983). "If higher education is to regulate itself more effectively, campus decision making must be improved" (Carnegie Foundation 1982, p. 74).

Suggested Institutional Approaches
Faculty, as do other professionals, insist upon being included in policy decisions that affect the manner in which they conduct their profession. Institutional attempts to respond to internal demands for accountability thus have the potential to antagonize faculty for two reasons: the ensuing limitation of traditional faculty autonomy and independence, and the limitation of the faculty's right to participate in making decisions that result in restricting faculty conduct.

Institutions cannot control the demands for accountability from federal and state governments, funding agencies, or the public itself. They can, however, influence the process used to respond to these demands by structuring the process by which faculty employment regulations are developed. In each of the examples of policies promulgated to limit faculty conduct cited earlier (restrictions on faculty/student interaction or university/industry relations, for example), a faculty committee developed the guidelines after careful deliberation. Administrators can assist these efforts by providing explicit descriptions of the requirements for accountability and suggesting the parameters within which institutional policies should be developed. Furthermore, legal counsel and information on academic freedom protections should be available to the faculty group charged with the responsibility of drafting guidelines for faculty conduct. At unionized institutions, the contract between the faculty and the administration may dictate that certain procedures be followed.

What is important in the development of these guidelines is that they must respond to the institution's mission and values as well as to external agents' requirements for accountability. Institutions and their faculty have been known to return grant funds or withdraw from federal contracts rather than comply with what they considered burdensome or inappropriate controls. It is important to both institutions and their faculty that the policy-making process and the resulting institutional regulations permit faculty to

weigh the receipt of external funding against its consequences for their professional autonomy and to make an informed choice between the two.

While many requirements for accountability result from "voluntary" relationships with external agencies (and thus can be avoided), some such requirements are *not* voluntary and are unavoidable. Sexual harassment is illegal under any circumstance, and the institution must provide leadership in the development and enforcement of guidelines to prevent and to punish such misbehavior. Similarly, reporting requirements for faculty workload tied to state funding are inevitable for colleges and universities, and reporting and accountability systems must be developed and monitored. Faculty participation in the policy process, however, will result in fairer procedures and enhanced faculty acceptance of limitations to their previous independence.

Colleges and universities are not isolated in this dilemma. Higher education associations like the Association of American Universities, the American Council on Education, and the American Association of University Professors have drafted policy statements on many of the issues addressed in this report—statements that leaders in higher education have pondered and discussed at length. While institutional circumstances differ, faculty and administrators attempting to resolve some of these issues should find these statements useful as a framework for campus discussion.

At a minimum, institutions that have not already done so should either use an existing faculty governance structure or create new faculty or faculty/administration committees to consider the following issues:

1. The institution's priorities in terms of academic programming, and the procedures to be used in the event that program reductions become necessary.
2. The definition of full-time faculty work and the institution's expectations for faculty productivity, both in quantitative and qualitative terms.
3. The institution's regulation of faculty contracts with private research sponsors, including prohibitions of restrictions on the type of research conducted, moratoria on publication, and other competitive concerns that limit a researcher's autonomy. The faculty may

wish to charge institutional review boards with oversight of the nature of faculty/industry relationships.

4. The regulation of faculty/student interaction and a fresh examination of the concept of "consensual" sexual relationships between faculty and students. Such deliberation should also include sanctions for misconduct involving students and a mechanism to ensure that the accused faculty member is afforded due process while the student is protected against retaliation.

5. Development of a system that can respond to charges of research fraud, with special attention to balancing collegial efforts to protect an accused researcher, on the one hand, against requirements for institutional accountability, especially when federal funds are involved, on the other.

6. Creation of an institutional policy toward intellectual products that neither overly rewards nor punishes researchers for engaging in research that results in patentable or otherwise lucrative research products.

7. Discussion of the creation and oversight of a system of faculty performance review, including attention to the role of the faculty in establishing review procedures, selecting review criteria, and conducting the review itself. Equally important are decisions about how the institution will use the results of the performance review.

8. Implementation of an ongoing dialogue among students, faculty, trustees, administrators, and the public about professional ethics, academic accountability, and academic freedom.

Academe has long been protected from external manipulation by both academic norms and by statutory and common law, preserving it as the place where ideas, no matter how unorthodox and no matter by whom espoused, may flourish. Although the academic profession values self-regulation as an important tenet of professional autonomy, its myriad connections with external forces, be they the government, the student consumer, or private industrial funding sources, have now increasingly brought the interests and concerns of those external agents into the academic enterprise. While the creators of the first statement on academic freedom may not have envisioned the complexity of the concerns against which academic freedom is matched today, they, like the framers of the Constitution, created a concept whose basic protections are unchanged, although its appreciation and interpretations have fluctuated over the years. The pressures for institutional accountability, which are more likely to expand than to contract over the next decade, suggest that faculty and administrators must continue to respond thoughtfully and wisely to balance academic freedom against the increasing demands for regulation of faculty by those who have a legitimate interest in the academic work product and thus the academic process.

REFERENCES

The ERIC Clearinghouse on Higher Education abstracts and indexes the current literature on higher education for the National Institute of Education's monthly bibliographic journal *Resources in Education*. Most of these publications are available through the ERIC Document Reproduction Service (EDRS). For publications cited in this bibliography that are available from EDRS, ordering number and price are included. Readers who wish to order a publication should write to the ERIC Document Reproduction Service, P.O. Box 190, Arlington, Virginia 22210. When ordering, please specify the document number. Documents are available as noted in microfiche (MF) and paper copy (PC). Because prices are subject to change, it is advisable to check the latest issue of *Resources in Education* for current cost based on the number of pages in the publication.

Books and Periodicals

Alexander, K. 1980. *School Law*. St. Paul, Minn.: West Publishing Co.

American Association of University Professors. 1916. "General Report of the Committee on Academic Freedom and Academic Tenure, 1915." *AAUP Bulletin* 1: 17–43.

———. 1977a. "Academic Freedom and Tenure: 1940 Statement of Principles and Interpretive Comments." *AAUP Policy Documents and Reports*. Washington, D.C.: AAUP.

———. 1977b. "Faculty Participation in the Selection and Retention of Administrators." *AAUP Policy Documents and Reports*. Washington, D.C.: AAUP. ED 136 646. 105 pp. MF–$1.17; PC–$11.12.

———. 1977c. "Procedural Standards in the Renewal or Nonrenewal of Faculty Appointments." *AAUP Policy Documents and Reports*. Washington, D.C.: AAUP. ED 136 646. 105 pp. MF–$1.17; PC–$11.12.

———. 1977d. "Statement of Procedural Standards for Faculty Dismissal Proceedings." *AAUP Policy Documents and Reports*. Washington, D.C.: AAUP. ED 136 646. 105 pp. MF–$1.17; PC–$11.12.

———. 1977e. "Statement on Professional Ethics." *AAUP Policy Documents and Reports*. Washington, D.C.: AAUP. ED 136 646. 105 pp. MF–$1.17; PC–$11.12.

Anderson, R. E. 1983. *Finance and Effectiveness: A Study of College Environments*. Princeton, N.J.: Educational Testing Service. ED 242 232. 193 pp. MF–$1.17; PC not available EDRS.

Association of American Medical Colleges. 1983. *The Maintenance of High Ethical Standards in the Conduct of Research*. Washington, D.C.: AAMC.

Association of American Universities. 1980. *Alternatives to A-21 Requirements for Documenting Salaries and Wages*. Report of the Ad Hoc Committee on Accountability. Washington, D.C.: AAU.

————. 1983. *Report of the Association of American Universities Committee on the Integrity of Research*. Washington, D.C.: AAU.

Association of American Universities, American Council on Education, and National Association of State Universities and Land-Grant Colleges. 1978. *Principles to Govern College and University Compensation Policies*. Ad Hoc Task Force on Faculty Compensation. Washington, D.C.: AAU, ACE, and NASULGC.

Astin, A. W. 1974. "Measuring the Outcomes of Higher Education." In *Evaluating Institutions for Accountability*, edited by H. R. Bowen. New Directions for Institutional Research No. 1. San Francisco: Jossey-Bass.

Austin, A. E., and Gamson, Z. F. 1983. *Academic Workplace: New Demands, Heightened Tensions*. ASHE-ERIC Higher Education Research Report No. 10. Washington, D.C.: Association for the Study of Higher Education. ED 243 397. 131 pp. MF–$1.17; PC–$12.87.

Bach, M. L., and Thornton, R. 1983. "Academic-Industrial Partnerships in Biomedical Research: Inevitability and Desirability." *Educational Record* 64: 26–32.

Baldridge, J. V.; Curtis, D. V.; Ecker, G. P.; and Riley, G. L. October 1978. "The Impact of Institutional Size and Complexity on Faculty Autonomy." *Journal of Higher Education* 44: 532–48.

Baldridge, J. V.; Kemerer, F. R.; and Associates. 1981. *Assessing the Impact of Faculty Collective Bargaining*. AAHE-ERIC Higher Education Research Report No. 8. Washington, D.C.: American Association for Higher Education. ED 216 653. 66 pp. MF–$1.17; PC–$7.24.

Baldwin, R. G., and Blackburn, R. T., eds. 1983. *College Faculty: Versatile Human Resources in a Period of Constraint*. New Directions for Institutional Research No. 40. San Francisco: Jossey-Bass.

Baratz, M. S. 1980. "Academic Tenure and Its Alternatives." *Phi Kappa Phi Journal* 60(2): 5–8.

Bennett, J. B., and Chater, S. S. 1984. "Evaluating the Performance of Tenured Faculty Members." *Educational Record* 65(2): 38–41.

Berdahl, R. O. 1971. *Statewide Coordination of Higher Education*. Washington, D.C.: American Council on Education.

Bess, J. L. 1981. *Intrinsic Satisfaction from Academic versus Other Professional Work*. Paper presented at the annual meeting of the Association for the Study of Higher Education, March, Washington, D.C. ED 203 805. 52 pp. MF–$1.17; PC–$7.24.

Binkley, M. A. 1979. *Analysis of Revised OMB Circular A-21*. NACUBO Special Report No. 79-7. Washington, D.C.: National Association of College and University Business Officers.

Bok, D. 1982. *Beyond the Ivory Tower: Social Responsibilities of the Modern University*. Cambridge, Mass.: Harvard University Press.

Bornheimer, D. G.; Burns, G. P.; and Dunke, G. S. 1973. *The Faculty in Higher Education*. Danville, Ill.: Interstate Printers and Publishers.

Boulding, K. E. 1975. "The Management of Decline." *Change* 7(5): 8–9 + .

Bouton, K. 11 September 1983. "Academic Research and Big Business: A Delicate Balance." *New York Times Magazine:* 62–63 + .

Bowen, H. R., ed. 1974. *Evaluating Institutions for Accountability*. New Directions for Institutional Research No. 1. San Francisco: Jossey-Bass.

———. 1978. *Academic Compensation: Are Faculty and Staff in American Higher Education Adequately Paid?* New York: Teachers Insurance and Annuity Association. ED 155 994. 139 pp. MF–$1.17; PC–$12.87.

———. September 1982. "Sharing the Effects: The Art of Retrenchment." *American Association for Higher Education Bulletin* 10: 12–13.

Broad, W. April 1981. "Fraud and the Structure of Science." *Science* 212: 137–39.

Broad, W., and Wade, N. 1982. *Betrayers of the Truth*. New York: Simon and Schuster.

Brookes, M. C. T., and German, K. L. 1983. *Meeting the Challenges: Developing Faculty Careers*. ASHE-ERIC Higher Education Research Report No. 3. Washington, D.C.: Association for the Study of Higher Education. ED 232 516. 54 pp. MF–$1.17; PC–$7.24.

Carnegie Council on Policy Studies in Higher Education. 1980. *Three Thousand Futures*. San Francisco: Jossey-Bass. ED 183 076. 175 pp. MF–$1.17; PC not available EDRS.

Carnegie Foundation for the Advancement of Teaching. 1982. *The Control of the Campus*. Lawrenceville, N.J.: Princeton University Press.

Centra, J. A. 1979. *Determining Faculty Effectiveness: Assessing Teaching, Research, and Service for Personnel Decisions and Improvements*. San Francisco: Jossey-Bass.

Chait, R. P., and Ford, A. T. 1982. *Beyond Traditional Tenure*. San Francisco: Jossey-Bass.

Chronicle of Higher Education. 27 June 1984. "University of Minnesota Toughens Policy on Harassment" 28: 2.

Colt, G. H. 1983. "Too Good to Be True." *Harvard Magazine:* 22–28 +.

Commission on Academic Tenure. 1973. *Faculty Tenure*. San Francisco: Jossey-Bass.

Crosson, P. H. 1983. *Public Service in Higher Education: Practices and Priorities*. ASHE-ERIC Higher Education Research Report No. 7. Washington, D.C.: Association for the Study of Higher Education. ED 239 569. 140 pp. MF–$1.17; PC–$12.87.

Daniels, R. D.; Martin, R. C.; Eisenberg, L.; Lewallen, J. M.; and Wright, R. A. 1977. *University-Connected Research Foundations: Characterizations and Analysis*. Norman, Okla.: University of Oklahoma.

Davidson, J. F. 1982. "Tenure, Governance, and Standards in the Academic Community." *Liberal Education* 68: 35–42.

Dill, D. D. 1982. "The Structure of the Academic Profession: Toward a Definition of Ethical Issues." *Journal of Higher Education* 53(3): 255–67.

Dillon, K. E. 1979. "Outside Professional Activities." *National Forum* 69(4): 38–42.

Dillon, K., and Bane, K. L. 1980. "Consulting and Conflict of Interest." *Educational Record* 61(4): 52–72.

Dillon, K. E., and Marsh, H. W. 1981. "Faculty Earnings Compared with Those of Nonacademic Professionals." *Journal of Higher Education* 52(6): 615–23.

Doi, J. I., ed. 1974. *Assessing Faculty Effort*. New Directions for Institutional Research No. 2. San Francisco: Jossey-Bass.

Dolan-Greene, C. 1981. "What If the Faculty Member to Be Laid Off Is the Governor's Brother?" In *Coping with Faculty Reductions*, edited by S. R. Hample. New Directions for Institutional Research No. 30. San Francisco: Jossey-Bass.

Dougherty, E. A. 1981. "Evaluating and Discontinuing Programs." In *Challenges of Retrenchment*, edited by J. R. Mingle and Associates. San Francisco: Jossey-Bass.

Dzeich, B. W., and Weiner, L. 1984. *The Lecherous Professor*. Boston: Beacon Press.

Eckert, R. E., and Williams, H. Y. 1972. *College Faculty View Themselves and Their Jobs*. Minneapolis, Minn.: University of Minnesota. ED 074 960. 64 pp. MF–$1.17; PC–$7.24.

Edwards, H. T., and Nordin, V. D. 1979. *Higher Education and the Law*. Cambridge, Mass.: Institute for Educational Management.

Finn, C. E., Jr. 1978. *Scholars, Dollars, and Bureaucrats*. Washington, D.C.: The Brookings Institution.

———. 1984. "Trying Higher Education." *Change* 16(4): 28–33+.

Folger, J. K., ed. 1977. *Increasing the Public Accountability of Higher Education*. New Directions for Institutional Research No. 16. San Francisco: Jossey-Bass.

Fowler, D. R. 1982–83. "University-Industry Research Relationships: The Research Agreement." *Journal of College and University Law* 9(4): 515–33.

Fuller, J. W., ed. 1983. *Issues in Faculty Personnel Policies.* New Directions for Higher Education No. 41. San Francisco: Jossey-Bass.

Fulton, O., and Trow, M. Winter 1974. "Research Activity in American Higher Education." *Sociology of Education* 47: 29–73.

Gideonse, H. D. 1950. "Changing Issues in Academic Freedom in the United States Today." *Proceedings of the American Philosophical Society* 94.

Gillmore, G. M. 1983–84. "Student Ratings as a Factor in Faculty Employment Decisions and Periodic Review." *Journal of College and University Law* 10(4): 557–76.

Glenny, L. A., and Bowen, F. M. 1981. "Warning Signals of Distress." In *Challenges of Retrenchment*, edited by J. R. Mingle and Associates. San Francisco: Jossey-Bass.

Gottschalk, E. C. 16 December 1982. "Some Frustrated Humanities Ph.D.'s Find Success after Being Retrained for Business." *Wall Street Journal*.

Hammond, M. F., and Tompkins, L. D. 1983. *A Major University's Response to a Mandated Budget Recession*. Paper presented at the annual conference of the Association for the Study of Higher Education, March, Washington, D.C.

Harvard Law Review. 1968. "Developments in the Law: Academic Freedom" 81: 1045–1150.

———. 1979. "Academic Freedom and Federal Regulation of University Hiring" 92: 879–97.

Henard, R. E. 1979. *The Impacts of the Faculty Workload Emphasis on Postsecondary Education in the 1980s*. Paper presented at the annual forum of the Association for Institutional Research, May, San Diego, Calif. ED 174 075. 21 pp. MF–$1.17; PC–$3.74.

Hendrickson, R. M., and Lee, B. A. 1983. *Academic Employment and Retrenchment: Judicial Review and Administrative*

Action. ASHE-ERIC Higher Education Research Report No. 8. Washington, D.C.: Association for the Study of Higher Education. ED 240 972. 133 pp. MF–$1.17; PC–$12.87.

Hobbs, W. C. 1978. *Government Regulation of Higher Education.* Cambridge, Mass.: Ballinger Publishing Co.

Hofstadter, R., and Metzger, W. P. 1955. *The Development of Academic Freedom in the United States.* New York: Columbia University Press.

Hoornstra, C. D., and Liethen, M. A. 1983–84. "Academic Freedom and Civil Discovery." *Journal of College and University Law* 10(2): 113–28.

Huther, J. W. 1974. "Faculty Workloads in the State Capital." In *Assessing Faculty Effort,* edited by J. I. Doi. New Directions for Institutional Research No. 2. San Francisco: Jossey-Bass.

Jacques, E. 1976. *A General Theory of Bureaucracy.* New York: Halstead Press.

Jedamus, P. 1974. "Teaching Loads over Time." In *Assessing Faculty Effort,* edited by J. I. Doi. New Directions for Institutional Research No. 2. San Francisco: Jossey-Bass.

Jensen, A. Fall 1983. "Taboo, Constraint, and Responsibility in Educational Research." *Journal of Social, Political, and Economic Studies* 8: 301–11.

Jensen, I., and Gutek, B. 1982. "Attribution and Assignment of Responsibility for Sexual Harassment." *Journal of Social Issues* 38(4): 121–36.

Johnson, J. October 1968. "The University as Problem Solver: Creativity and the Ghetto." *Liberal Education* 54: 421–28.

Jolly, D. 1978. *Perspective of California Legislators on Disclosure and Accountability as It Relates to Faculty Salaries and Supplemental Income.* Paper presented at the Third Annual Academic Planning Conference, University of Southern California, January, Los Angeles, Calif. ED 152 166. 10 pp. MF–$1.17; PC–$3.74.

Joughin, L. 1967a. "Academic Due Process." In *Academic Freedom and Tenure,* edited by L. Joughin. Madison: University of Wisconsin Press.

———, ed. 1967b. *Academic Freedom and Tenure.* Madison: University of Wisconsin Press.

Kaplin, W. 1978. *The Law of Higher Education.* San Francisco: Jossey-Bass.

Kerr, C. 1984. *Survival in the 1980s: Quality, Mission, and Financing Options.* Tucson, Ariz.: Center for the Study of Higher Education, University of Arizona. ED 236 994. 296 pp. MF–$1.17; PC not available EDRS.

Lachs, P. S. 1983–84. "University Patent Policy." *Journal of College and University Law* 10(3): 263–92.

Ladd, E. C., Jr. 1979. "The Work Experience of American College Professors: Some Data and an Argument." In *Faculty Career Development*. Current Issues in Higher Education No. 2. Washington, D.C.: American Association for Higher Education. ED 193 998. 44 pp. MF–$1.17; PC not available EDRS.

Ladd, E. C., Jr., and Lipset, S. M. 1975. *The Divided Academy: Professors and Politics*. New York: McGraw-Hill.

———. 1977. *Survey of the American Professoriate*. Storrs, Conn.: University of Connecticut.

Lee, B. A. 1978. *Collective Bargaining in Four-Year Colleges*. AAHE-ERIC Higher Education Research Report No. 5. Washington, D.C.: American Association for Higher Education. ED 162 542. 85 pp. MF–$1.17; PC–$9.37.

Lee, B. A. In press. "Federal Court Involvement in Academic Decision Making: Impact on Peer Review." *Journal of Higher Education*.

Lee, B. A., and Olswang, S. G. Forthcoming. "The Parameters of the Faculty Employment Relationship." In *Higher Education: Handbook of Theory and Research,* edited by J. Smart. New York: Agathon Press.

Linnell, R. H., ed. 1982. *Dollars and Scholars*. Los Angeles: University of Southern California Press.

Lovain, T. 1983–84. "Grounds for Dismissing Tenured Postsecondary Faculty for Cause." *Journal of College and University Law* 10(3): 419–33.

Lovett, C. M. 1980. *Different Journey: Senior Academics and Career Change*. New York: Baruch College, City University of New York.

McGuiness, A. C., Jr. 1981. "The Federal Government and Postsecondary Education." In *Higher Education in American Society,* edited by P. G. Altbach and R. O. Berdahl. Buffalo, N.Y.: Prometheus Books.

Machlup, F. 1967a. "In Defense of Academic Tenure." In *Academic Freedom and Tenure,* edited by L. Joughin. Madison: University of Wisconsin Press.

———. 1967b. "On Some Misconceptions Concerning Academic Freedom." In *Academic Freedom and Tenure,* edited by L. Joughin. Madison: University of Wisconsin Press.

Magarrell, J. 10 November 1982. "Decline in Faculty Morale Laid to Governance Role, not Salary." *Chronicle of Higher Education* 27: 1.

Marcus, L. R.; Leone, A. O.; and Goldberg, E. D. 1983. *The Path to Excellence: Quality Assurance in Higher Education.* ASHE-ERIC Higher Education Research Report No. 1. Washington, D.C.: Association for the Study of Higher Education. ED 227 800. 76 pp. MF–$1.17; PC–$9.37.

Marks, R., and Cathcart, H. 1974. "Discipline within the Legal Profession: Is It Self-Regulation?" *University of Illinois Law Forum, 1974:* 193–218.

Marsh, H. W., and Dillon, K. E. September/October 1980. "Academic Productivity and Faculty Supplemental Income." *Journal of Higher Education* 51: 546–55.

Meléndez, W. A., and de Guzmán, R. M. 1983. *Burnout: The New Academic Disease.* ASHE-ERIC Higher Education Research Report No. 9. Washington, D.C.: Association for the Study of Higher Education. ED 242 255. 114 pp. MF–$1.17; PC–$11.12.

Metzger, W. P. 1955. *Academic Freedom in the Age of the University.* New York: Columbia University Press.

———. 1977. *The American Concept of Academic Freedom in Formation.* New York: Arno Press.

———. 1979. "The History of Tenure." In *Tenure.* Current Issues in Higher Education No. 6. Washington, D.C.: American Association for Higher Education. ED 194 002. 21 pp. MF–$1.17; PC not available EDRS.

Miller, R. 1981. "The Role of Academic Freedom in Defining the Faculty Employment Contract." *Case Western Reserve Law Review* 31: 608–55.

Miller, R. I. 1972. *Evaluating Faculty Performance.* San Francisco: Jossey-Bass.

Millett, J. D. 1981. "State Government." In *Higher Education in American Society,* edited by P. G. Altbach and R. O. Berdahl. Buffalo, N.Y.: Prometheus Books.

———. 1984. *Conflict in Higher Education.* San Francisco: Jossey-Bass.

Mingle, J. R., and Associates, eds. 1981. *Challenges of Retrenchment.* San Francisco: Jossey-Bass.

Mishkin, B. 1983. "Responding to Allegations of Scientific Misconduct: Pratfalls, Pitfalls, and Prophylaxis." *National Association of College and University Attorneys College Digest* 13: 215–22.

Mortimer, K. P. 1981. "Procedures and Criteria for Faculty Retrenchment." In *Challenges of Retrenchment,* edited by J. R. Mingle and Associates. San Francisco: Jossey-Bass.

Mortimer, K. P., and Lozier, G. G. 1974a. "Collective Bargaining: Implications for Governance." In *Insights into Higher Education: Selected Writings of CSHE, 1969–73.* University

Park, Pa.: Center for the Study of Higher Education. ED 067
059. 69 pp. MF–$1.17; PC–$7.24.

———. 1974b. "Faculty Workload and Collective Bargaining." In
Assessing Faculty Effort, edited by J. I. Doi. New Directions
for Institutional Research No. 2. San Francisco: Jossey-Bass.

Murphy, W. P. 1963. "Academic Freedom: An Emerging Constitutional Right." *Law and Contemporary Problems* 28: 447–86.

Neuman, F. September 1982. "Selecting the Effects: The Priorities of Retrenchment." *American Association for Higher Education Bulletin* 10: 11–13.

Nisbet, R. 1978. "The Future of Tenure." *Change* 10: 27.

Noble, D. S., and Pfund, N.E. 1980. "Business Goes Back to
College." *The Nation* 231: 233.

Oakes. 1978. *Lawyer and Judge: The Ethical Duty of Compe-
tency in Ethics and Advocacy.* Final report of the 1978 Annual
Chief Justice Earl Warren Conference on Advocacy in the
United States, Washington, D.C.

Olswang, S. G. 1982–83. "Planning the Unthinkable: Issues in
Institutional Reorganization and Faculty Reductions." *Journal
of College and University Law* 9(4): 431–49.

Olswang, S. G., and Fantel, J. I. 1980–81. "Tenure and Periodic
Performance Review: Compatible Legal and Administrative
Principles." *Journal of College and University Law* 7(1–2):
1–30.

Olswang, S. G., and Lee, B.A. 1984. "Scientific Misconduct:
Institutional Procedures and Due Process Considerations."
Journal of College and University Law 11(1): 51–64.

O'Toole, J. P. 1979. "A Conscientious Objection." In *Tenure.*
New Rochelle, N.Y.: Change Magazine Press.

Palmer, D. D., and Patton, C. V. 1981. "Mid-Career Change
Options in Academe: Experience and Possibilities." *Journal of
Higher Education* 52: 378–98.

Palmer, J. 1974. "Patents and University Research." *Law and
Contemporary Problems* 12: 680–97.

Patton, C. V. 1983. "Institutional Practices and Faculty Who
Leave." In *College Faculty: Versatile Human Resources in a
Period of Constraint,* edited by R. G. Baldwin and R. T. Black-
burn. New Directions for Institutional Research No. 40. San
Francisco: Jossey-Bass.

Perry, S. 23 March 1983. "Sexual Harassment on the Campuses:
Deciding Where to Draw the Line." *Chronicle of Higher Education* 27: 21–22.

Peterson, M. W.; Ervin, J.; and Wilson, R. 1977. "State-Level
Performance Budgeting." In *Increasing the Public Accountability of Higher Education,* edited by J. Folger. New Direc-

tions for Institutional Research No. 16. San Francisco: Jossey-Bass.

Powers, D. R., and Powers, M. F. 1983. *Making Participatory Management Work*. San Francisco: Jossey-Bass.

Rich, H. E., and Jolicoeur, P. M. 1978. "Faculty Role Perceptions and Preferences in the Seventies." *Sociology of Work and Occupations* 5(4): 423–45.

Rich, S. L., and Brown, B. R. 1976. *Survey of Institutional Policies Regarding Compensated External Activities of Faculty*. Technical Memorandum No. TM-76-1. Louisville, Ky.: Office of Institutional Research, University of Louisville.

Romney, L. C. 1971. *Faculty Activity Analysis: Overview and Major Issues*. Boulder, Colo.: Western Interstate Commission for Higher Education. ED 062 947. 117 pp. MF–$1.17; PC–$11.12.

Rose, H. C., Jr., and Hample, S. R. 1981. "Conclusion: Developing a Process to Deal with Potential Faculty Reduction." In *Coping with Faculty Reductions,* edited by S. R. Hample. New Directions for Institutional Research No. 34. San Francisco: Jossey-Bass.

Rudolph, F. R. 1962. *The American College and University*. New York: Vintage Books.

Sanger, D. E. 21 August 1983. "University of California Puts Limits on Private Research Pacts." *New York Times*.

Schurr, G. M. 1982. "Toward a Code of Ethics for Academics." *Journal of Higher Education* 53(3): 318–34.

Seldin, P. 1980. *Successful Faculty Evaluation Programs*. Creigers, N.Y.: Coventry Press.

Shapiro, H. T. 1982. "The Privilege and the Responsibility: Some Reflections on the Nature, Function, and Future of Academic Tenure." *Academe* 69: 3a–7a.

Shils, E. 1983. *The Academic Ethic*. Chicago: University of Chicago Press.

Shulman, C. H. 1973. *Employment of Nontenured Faculty: Some Implications of* Roth *and* Sindermann. AAHE-ERIC Higher Education Research Report No. 8. Washington, D.C.: American Association for Higher Education. ED 084 994. 75 pp. MF–$1.17; PC–$7.24.

———. 1978. *Compliance with Federal Regulations: At What Cost?* AAHE-ERIC Higher Education Research Report No. 6. Washington, D.C.: American Association for Higher Education. ED 165 552. 59 pp. MF–$1.17; PC–$7.24.

———. 1979. *Old Expectations, New Realities: The Academic Profession Revisited*. AAHE-ERIC Higher Education Research Report No. 2. Washington, D.C.: American Association

for Higher Education. ED 169 874. 58 pp. MF–$1.17; PC–
$7.24.

———. 1980a. "Do Faculty Really Work that Hard?" *AAHE
Bulletin* 32(2): 5–12. ED 192 668. 5 pp. MF–$1.17; PC–$3.74.

———. 1980b. "Faculty Ethics: New Dilemmas, New Choices."
AAHE Bulletin 31: 7–10. ED 187 290. 5 pp. MF–$1.17; PC–
$3.74.

———. 1981. "That Wonderful 12-Hour Work Week."*AGB Reports* 23(2):15–19.

Silber, J. R. 1973. "Tenure in Context." In *The Tenure Debate*,
edited by B. L. Smith and Associates. San Francisco: Jossey-
Bass.

Slaughter, S. March 1980. "The Danger Zone: Academic Freedom and Civil Liberties." *Annals of the American Academy of
Political and Social Science* 448:46–61.

———. 1981. "Political Action, Faculty Autonomy, and Retrenchment: A Decade of Academic Freedom, 1970–1980." In
Higher Education in American Society, edited by P. G. Altbach
and R. O. Berdahl. Buffalo, N.Y.: Prometheus Books.

Smith, A. A. 1981–82. "Implications of the Uniform Patent Leg-
islation to Colleges and Universities." *Journal of College and
University Law* 8(1):82–96.

Smith, A. B. 1976. *Faculty Development and Evaluation in
Higher Education.* AAHE-ERIC Higher Education Research
Report No. 8. Washington, D.C.: American Association for
Higher Education. ED 132 891. 85 pp. MF–$1.17;PC–$9.37.

Solomon, L. C. 1981. *Underemployed Ph.D.'s.* Lexington,
Mass.: Lexington Books.

Somers, A. 1982. "Sexual Harassment in Academe: Legal Issues
and Definitions." *Journal of Social Issues* 38(4):23–32.

Stanford University. 1977. "Policy on Consulting by Members of
the Academic Council: Principles and General Standards."
Palo Alto, Calif.: Stanford University.

Statement from the Biotechnology Conference at Pajaro Dunes.
March 1982.

Stecklein, J. E. 1974. "Approaches to Measuring Workload over
the Past Two Decades." In *Assessing Faculty Effort*, edited by
J. I. Doi. New Directions for Institutional Research No. 2. San
Francisco: Jossey-Bass.

Stroup, K. 1983. "Faculty Evaluation." In *Issues in Faculty
Personnel Policies*, edited by J. W. Fuller. New Directions for
Higher Education No. 41. San Francisco: Jossey-Bass.

Tatel, D., and Guthrie, R. C. 1983. "The Legal Ins and Outs of
University-Industry Collaboration." *Educational Record*
64:19–25.

Thompson, R. K. 1971. "How Does the Faculty Spend Its Time?" Mimeographed. Seattle: University of Washington.

Tucker, A., and Mautz, R. B. 1982. "Academic Freedom, Tenure, and Incompetence." *Educational Record* 63:22–25.

Van Alstyne, W. 1970. "The Constitutional Rights of Teachers and Professors." *Duke University Law Journal* 1969:841–67.

Waggaman, J. S. 1983. *Faculty Recruitment, Retention, and Fair Employment: Obligations and Opportunities.* ASHE-ERIC Higher Education Research Report No. 2. Washington, D.C.: Association for the Study of Higher Education. ED 227 806. 73 pp. MF–$1.17; PC–$7.24.

Wallhaus, R. A., ed. 1975. *Measuring and Increasing Academic Productivity.* New Directions for Institutional Research No. 8. San Francisco: Jossey-Bass.

Webb, F. 1983. "Inspirer or Perspirer: Who Gets the Glory When the Study Ends?"*American Psychological Association Monitor* 14(2):4–6.

Weeks, K. M. 1979. "Dismissal for Cause." *AGB Reports* 21(3):18–22.

White, W. 1980. *Managing Personnel and Organizational Stress in Institutions of Higher Education.* Rockville, Md.: N.C.S., Inc.

Wieruszowski, H. 1966. *The Medieval University.* New York: Van Nostrand Reinhold Company.

Williams, D. T., Jr.; Olswang, S. G.; and Hargett, G. H. In press. "A Matter of Degree: Faculty Morale as a Function of Involvement in Institutional Decisions during Times of Financial Crisis." *Review of Higher Education.*

Willie, R., and Stecklein, J. E. 1981. *A Three-Decade Comparison of College Faculty Characteristics, Satisfactions, Activities, and Attitudes.* Paper presented at the annual forum of the Association for Institutional Research, Minneapolis, Minn. ED 205 113. 25 pp. MF–$1.17; PC–$3.74.

Winerip, M. 6 March 1984. "Academic Freedom Tenet Is Tested." *New York Times.*

Woytash, J. 1978. "It's Time to Do Something about Lawyer Competence." *American Bar Association Journal* 64:308–10.

Yale University. 1983. *Policy Statement on Collaborative Research.* New Haven, Conn.: Yale University.

Yuker, H. E. 1974. *Faculty Workload: Facts, Myths, and Commentary.* AAHE-ERIC Higher Education Research Report No. 6. Washington, D.C.: American Association for Higher Education. ED 095 756. 70 pp. MF–$1.17; PC–$7.24.

Zimic, L. F. 1978. "Breach of Responsibility in Extramural Utterances." *Educational Record* 59(1):45–60.

Cases

Adamian v. *Jacobsen*, 523 F.2d 929 (9th Cir. 1975).

Alexander v. *Yale University*, 631 F.2d 178 (2d Cir. 1980).

American Association of University Professors v. *Bloomfield College*, 129 N.J. Super. 249, 322 A.2d 846 (1974).

Application of Schlitter, 234 F.2d 882 (C.C.P.A. 1956).

Bates v. *Sponberg*, 547 F.2d 325 (6th Cir. 1976).

Bignall v. *North Idaho College*, 538 F.2d 243 (9th Cir. 1976).

Board of Regents v. *Roth*, 408 U.S. 564 (1972).

Board of Trustees of Mount San Antonio Junior College v. *Hartman*, 55 Cal. Rptr. 144 (Ct. App. 1966).

Board of Trustees v. *Stubblefield*, 94 Cal. Rptr. 318 (Ct. App. 1971).

Browzin v. *Catholic University*, 527 F.2d 843 (D.C. Cir. 1975).

Chitwood v. *Feaster*, 468 F.2d 359 (4th Cir. 1972).

Chung v. *Park*, 514 F.2d 382 (3d Cir. 1975).

Diamond v. *Diehr*, 450 U.S. 175 (1981).

Dow Chemical Co. v. *Allen*, 672 F.2d 1262 (7th Cir. 1982).

Endress v. *Brookdale Community College*, 364 A.2d 1080 (N.J. Super. A.D. 1976).

Ferguson v. *Thomas*, 430 F.2d 852 (5th Cir. 1970).

Gottschalk v. *Benson*, 409 U.S. 63 (1972).

Greene v. *Howard University*, 412 F.2d 1128 (D.C. Cir. 1969).

Gross v. *University of Tennessee*, 448 F. Supp. 245 (W.D. Tenn. 1978), *aff'd*, 620 F.2d 109 (6th Cir. 1980).

Hetrick v. *Martin*, 480 F.2d 705 (6th Cir. 1973).

Jawa v. *Fayetteville State University*, 426 F. Supp. 218 (E.D.N.C. 1976).

Keddie v. *Pennsylvania State University*, 412 F. Supp. 1264 (M.D. Pa. 1976).

Keyishian v. *Board of Regents*, 385 U.S. 589 (1967).

Krotkoff v. *Goucher College*, 585 F.2d 675 (4th Cir. 1978).

Lehmann v. *Board of Trustees of Whitman College*, 89 Wash. 2d 874, 576 P.2d 397 (1978).

Levitt v. *Board of Trustees of Nebraska State College*, 376 F. Supp. 945 (D. Neb. 1974).

Mt. Healthy v. *Doyle*, 419 U.S. 274 (1977).

NLRB v. *Yeshiva University*, 444 U.S. 672 (1980).

Shaw v. *Board of Trustees of Frederick Community College*, 549 F.2d 929 (4th Cir. 1976).

Smith v. *Losee*, 485 F.2d 334 (10th Cir. 1973).

Spaulding v. *University of Washington*, 740 F.2d 686 (9th Cir. 1984).

Stastny v. *Board of Trustees of Central Washington University*, 647 P.2d 496 (Wash. App. 1982).

Sweezy v. *New Hampshire*, 354 U.S. 234 (1957).

Toney v. *Reagan*, 467 F.2d 953 (9th Cir. 1972).

Trustees of Dartmouth College v. *Woodward*, 4 Wheat. (U.S.) 518 (1819).

White v. *Board of Trustees of Western Wyoming Community College*, 648 P.2d 528 (Wyo. 1982).

Wood v. *University of Tulsa* (Ct. App. Okla. No. 53,230, March 17, 1981).

Statutes and Regulations

The Animal Welfare Act of 1970, 7 U.S.C. §2131 (1982), 9 CFR §2.1 (1983).

The Copyright Act, 17 U.S.C. 101.

Equal Employment Opportunity Commission, *Interpretive Guideline on Discrimination because of Sex under Title VII*, 29 CFR 1604.11.

Guidelines for Research Involving Recombinant DNA Molecules, 48 Fed. Reg. 24556 (1983).

Office of Management and Budget, *Circular A-21*, "Cost Principles for Educational Universities," 44 Fed. Reg. 12368 et seq.

Patent and Trademark Amendments of 1980 (P.L. 96–517).

45 CFR §76 (1983).

45 CFR §46.101–.409 (1983).

ASHE-ERIC HIGHER EDUCATION RESEARCH REPORTS

Starting in 1983, the Association for the Study of Higher Education assumed cosponsorship of the Higher Education Research Reports with the ERIC Clearinghouse on Higher Education. For the previous 11 years, ERIC and the American Association for Higher Education prepared and published the reports.

Each report is the definitive analysis of a tough higher education problem, based on a thorough research of pertinent literature and institutional experiences. Report topics, identified by a national survey, are written by noted practitioners and scholars with prepublication manuscript reviews by experts.

Ten monographs in the ASHE-ERIC Higher Education Research Report series are published each year, available individually or by subscription. Subscription to 10 issues is $55 regular; $40 for members of AERA, AAHE, and AIR; $35 for members of ASHE. (Add $7.50 outside U.S.)

Prices for single copies, including 4th class postage and handling, are $7.50 regular and $6.00 for members of AERA, AAHE, AIR, and ASHE. If faster 1st class postage is desired for U.S. and Canadian orders, for each publication ordered add $.75; for overseas, add $4.50. For VISA and MasterCard payments, give card number, expiration date, and signature. Orders under $25 must be prepaid. Bulk discounts are available on orders of 10 or more of a single title. Order from the Publications Department, Association for the Study of Higher Education, One Dupont Circle, Suite 630, Washington, D.C. 20036, (202) 296-2597. Write for a complete list of Higher Education Research Reports and other ASHE and ERIC publications.

1981 Higher Education Research Reports

1. Minority Access to Higher Education
   Jean L. Preer

2. Institutional Advancement Strategies in Hard Times
   Michael D. Richards and Gerald Sherratt

3. Functional Literacy in the College Setting
   Richard C. Richardson, Jr., Kathryn J. Martens, and Elizabeth C. Fisk

4. Indices of Quality in the Undergraduate Experience
   George D. Kuh

5. Marketing in Higher Education
   Stanley M. Grabowski

6. Computer Literacy in Higher Education
   Francis E. Masat

7. Financial Analysis for Academic Units
   Donald L. Walters

8. Assessing the Impact of Faculty Collective Bargaining
   J. Victor Baldridge, Frank R. Kemerer, and Associates

9. Strategic Planning, Management, and Decision Making
   Robert G. Cope

10. Organizational Communication in Higher Education
    Robert D. Gratz and Philip J. Salem

1982 Higher Education Research Reports

1. Rating College Teaching: Criterion Studies of Student Evaluation-of-Instruction Instruments
   Sidney E. Benton

2. Faculty Evaluation: The Use of Explicit Criteria for Promotion, Retention, and Tenure
   Neal Whitman and Elaine Weiss

3. The Enrollment Crisis: Factors, Actors, and Impacts
   J. Victor Baldridge, Frank R. Kemerer, and Kenneth C. Green

4. Improving Instruction: Issues and Alternatives for Higher Education
   Charles C. Cole, Jr.

5. Planning for Program Discontinuance: From Default to Design
   Gerlinda S. Melchiori

6. State Planning, Budgeting, and Accountability: Approaches for Higher Education
   Carol E. Floyd

7. The Process of Change in Higher Education Institutions
   Robert C. Nordvall

8. Information Systems and Technological Decisions: A Guide for Non-Technical Administrators
   Robert L. Bailey

9. Government Support for Minority Participation in Higher Education
   Kenneth C. Green

10. The Department Chair: Professional Development and Role Conflict
    David B. Booth

1983 Higher Education Research Reports

1. The Path to Excellence: Quality Assurance in Higher Education
   Laurence R. Marcus, Anita O. Leone, and Edward D. Goldberg

2. Faculty Recruitment, Retention, and Fair Employment: Obligations and Opportunities
   John S. Waggaman

3. Meeting the Challenges: Developing Faculty Careers
   Michael C. T. Brookes and Katherine L. German

4. Raising Academic Standards: A Guide to Learning Improvement
   Ruth Talbott Keimig

5. Serving Learners at a Distance: A Guide to Program Practices
   Charles E. Feasley

6. Competence, Admissions, and Articulation: Returning to the Basics in Higher Education
   Jean L. Preer

7. Public Service in Higher Education: Practices and Priorities
   Patricia H. Crosson

8. Academic Employment and Retrenchment: Judicial Review and Administrative Action
   Robert M. Hendrickson and Barbara A. Lee

9. Burnout: The New Academic Disease
   Winifred Albizu Meléndez and Rafael M. de Guzmán

10. Academic Workplace: New Demands, Heightened Tensions
    Ann E. Austin and Zelda F. Gamson

1984 Higher Education Research Reports

1. Adult Learning: State Policies and Institutional Practices
   K. Patricia Cross and Anne-Marie McCartan

2. Student Stress: Effects and Solutions
   Neal A. Whitman, David C. Spendlove, and Claire H. Clark

3. Part-time Faculty: Higher Education at a Crossroads
   Judith M. Gappa

4. Sex Discrimination Law in Higher Education: The Lessons of the Past Decade
   J. Ralph Lindgren, Patti T. Ota, Perry A. Zirkel, and Nan Van Gieson

5. Faculty Freedoms and Institutional Accountability: Interactions and Conflicts
   Steven G. Olswang and Barbara A. Lee